The Understanding of Christian Faith

The Understanding of Christian Faith

Schubert M. Ogden

CASCADE *Books* · Eugene, Oregon

THE UNDERSTANDING OF CHRISTIAN FAITH

Cascade Books
An Imprint of Wipf and Stock Publishers
199 W. 8th Ave., Suite 3
Eugene, OR 97401

www.wipfandstock.com

ISBN 13: 978-1-60899-326-0

Cataloging-in-Publication data:

Ogden, Schubert Miles, 1928–.

    The understanding of Christian faith / Schubert M. Ogden.

    xii + 168 p. ; 23 cm. — Includes bibliographical references and indexes.

    ISBN 13: 978-1-60899-326-0

    1. Theology, doctrinal—Introductions. 2. Theology. I. Title.

BT65 O35 2010

Manufactured in the U.S.A.

To my students

True fidelity to tradition does not consist in canonizing a certain stage of history. It is, indeed, always criticism of the present before the forum of tradition; but it is also always criticism of tradition before the forum of the present. True fidelity is not going back but going on.

True fidelity is never 'archaizing repetition,' but always and only critical appropriation, which makes the legitimate motives of the tradition one's own and brings them to expression in a new form.

—Rudolf Bultmann

Contents

Contents

Preface

THE TITLE OF THIS book has been chosen to take advantage of its ambiguity. Being a genitive phrase, "the understanding of Christian faith" may be read to mean either of two things: the understanding of which Christian faith is the subject, which forms its own content as Christian faith; or the understanding of which it itself, in its understanding, is the object, which consists in the critical appropriation of its content and which, as I argue, is the proper business of Christian systematic theology. I hope, accordingly, that readers will keep both understandings in mind in working through my argument.

I also hope that they will take my book for what it is, and not for what it isn't. More than an essay, or a study, or a collection thereof, it is also less than the multi-volumed systematic theology that theologians such as myself are not unreasonably expected to write. Both in scope and in level and extent of argument, it is more like the introductory courses I offered during most of the some forty years I regularly taught Christian systematic theology. In fact, it has its origins in the lectures I wrote and constantly rewrote for those courses, and the readers I have mainly had in mind in writing it are students of theology very much like those to whom I have taken the liberty of dedicating it. Another way of saying this is that the book I have tried to write is the book I myself could wish I had had early on in my own formation as a professional theologian.

I will be more than pleased, of course, should it prove helpful to others as well, particularly any lay theologians such as I have had the privilege of working with throughout my teaching career. I know from long experience that there are many more such persons both within the churches and outside them than ever receive the theological education that would enable them to do the theology they are able and willing to do.

I would say three further things I hope my readers will find helpful. The first is that, next to the writings of the New Testament and the theological work of a few of my contemporaries, probably the most important factor in shaping the structure of my theological understanding has been Protestant orthodox theology. By "structure" here I mean, first of all, the basic questions, or topics, with which I as a Christian systematic theologian have felt obliged to deal. But I also mean the critically reflective way in which I have found myself having to deal with them, which places a high premium on clarifying concepts, analyzing necessary presuppositions and implications and, above all, developing and assessing the arguments required to support conclusions. Therefore, for all of the vast difference in content between Protestant orthodoxy and my kind of liberal—or, as I prefer to say, revisionary—theology, I suspect nothing would more conduce to understanding how and why I am about what I am about than also becoming acquainted with such books as (in their English translations) Heinrich Heppe, *Reformed Dogmatics: Set Out and Illustrated from the Sources,* and especially Heinrich Schmid, *The Doctrinal Theology of the Evangelical Lutheran Church.* More than that, I am confident that few things would contribute as much to anyone's becoming a well-furnished systematic theologian as getting to know just such handy summaries of classical Christian thought. Happily, both books have only recently become available again in new paperback editions.

A second thing I want to say is that, from early in my career as a theologian, I have only grown in my agreement with the Anglican bishop in the seventeenth century who sagely remarked that "the most useful of all books in theology would be one with the title *De Paucitate Credendorum,* on the fewness of the things which a man must believe."[1] Of course, even more useful would be a book that actually delivered on the promise implied by such a title. In any case, I have done my best in this book to make clear that, although there are indeed many Christian beliefs, they are really all ways of expressing only one Christian belief, only one understanding of the ultimate meaning of human existence. Therefore, I shall only be grateful if my readers are struck, finally, by the essential simplicity of the understanding of Christian faith itself—not only of my poor attempt to understand it.

The third thing I would say is that the understanding of Christian faith (*gen. obj.*) set forth in this book is, in all essentials, the understanding for and from which I have argued in all of my earlier books and other published writings. Therefore, readers may well find in them further,

1. Quoted by Inge, *Things New and Old,* 48.

amplifying discussions of many of the topics and questions dealt with, or touched on, in the following chapters. This may prove especially so in the case of the foundational topics of God and of Jesus Christ, which are the specific subjects respectively of my books, *The Reality of God* and *The Point of Christology*. But my guess is that some readers, at least, may particularly welcome further discussion of an important issue not gone into here—namely, the whole issue of the Christian understanding of non-Christian religions, which I have considered at some length in my book, *Is There Only One True Religion or Are There Many?*

There remains the happy duty of remembering those who have been of particular help in completing the book. I am most especially obliged to three of my close colleagues and friends who know my work well and were good enough to read the entire typescript and give me their critical responses: Philip E. Devenish, Franklin I. Gamwell, and Andrew D. Scrimgeour. Although I have not followed all of their suggestions, I know that it is a much better book than it would have been had I not had the benefit of their criticisms, and that I alone am responsible for such inadequacies as remain. To each of them, I express my heartfelt thanks for only this latest proof of their old and abiding support and affection.

I would also express my gratitude to the publisher of the *Union Seminary Quarterly Review*, who has granted permission to make use of material from an essay of mine originally appearing in its pages, viz., "The Meaning of Christian Hope," copyright © 1975.

Rollinsville, Colorado
November 2009

1

Prolegomena: On Theology

1.0. PRELIMINARY REMARKS

ONE OF THE DEFINING characteristics of theology, which it shares with philosophy in contrast to special sciences such as biology or physics, is that it necessarily includes reflection on itself and its own conditions of possibility as a form of critical reflection. Thus the question, "What is theology?" is itself a theological question whose answer is subject to the same conditions of adequacy as any other theological answer. This means that the treatment of so-called prolegomena, in which theologians have commonly tried to answer this question, together with a range of other closely connected questions, itself belongs to theology, rather than to some other field or discipline, such as philosophy, in which one first has to become involved before one can undertake to do theology proper. Etymology to the contrary, then, I entirely agree with Karl Barth when he says that the word "prolegomena" cannot rightly mean the things that are said *before* one does theology, but only the things that are said *first,* once one is already doing it.

Of course, what is *said* first in a formal presentation such as this may very well not be what is *done* first. Quite commonly, in fact, we find ourselves engaged in doing a certain thing long before we explicitly ask and answer the question, "What, exactly, am I doing?" or "What is it to do it?" But if the question, "What is it to do theology?" is itself a theological question, we cannot clarify what it means to ask it except by answering it; and we cannot possibly answer it except by doing the very thing it asks about doing. We must do theology ourselves if we are to ask theologically what it is to do it.

There are, in any case, good reasons to begin any undertaking by trying to understand as best one can what is to be undertaken and how one is to go about it. And so, in this discussion of prolegomena, I propose to speak to the question, "What is theology?" understood to mean, What is it to do theology? In developing an answer to this question, I hope to throw light on two more specific questions: (1) What is there for theology to do?—or, in other words, What is the distinctive *task* (or *tasks*) of theology? and (2) How is it to be done?—which is to say, what is the proper *method* (or *methods*) of theology? I shall develop my answers to these questions in three main sections, dealing in turn with (1) theology in general; (2) Christian theology in particular; and (3) Christian systematic theology.

1.1.THEOLOGY IN GENERAL

Literally, "theology" means *logos* about *theos*, or as we may say in ordinary English, thought and/or speech about God. And this is as good an initial definition of the term as one could want.

But only a little reflection makes clear that it can and should be broadened, since the same human questions to which thought and/or speech about God serve to give answers can also be asked and answered, not by thinking and/or speaking about God, but by thinking and/or speaking about something else instead—e.g., Nature, the Absolute, the Real Self, the Whole, Nirvana, the One, or the Form of the Good. The term "God" itself can, of course, be used so broadly that it means simply ultimate reality in its meaning for us, whatever this meaning may prove to be, or—to speak less existentially and more metaphysically—it may mean ultimate reality in its structure in itself, however we may finally conceive its structure. But if "God" is used, as it ordinarily is, in some stricter, specifically theistic sense, the questions it serves to answer may also be answered by thinking and/or speaking about any number of things other than God.

At the same time, reflection also makes clear that the initial definition is, in another respect, not too narrow but too broad, and therefore also needs to be narrowed. "Theology," as it has come to be commonly used, does not mean *all* thought and/or speech about God, or ultimate reality, but only *some* of it—namely, such as is involved in either the process or the product of more or less critically appropriating all the rest of it, which remainder we may call "witness," rather than "theology."

If we take account of both of these reflections, theology in general may be defined as *the thought and/or speech involved in critically appropriating witness by critically interpreting its meaning and critically validating its claims to validity*, which is to say, the claims that witness itself makes or implies simply as and because it is witness. By "witness," then, I mean all the rest of our thinking and/or speaking (including all our doing as well as our saying) about either God or the ultimate reality about which "God" itself is but one of many ways of thinking and/or speaking.

But if what is properly meant by "God," or "ultimate reality," is what could not fail to be real if anything else is so much as possible, then whatever we as human beings think, say, or do about anything at all must be at least implicitly about God or ultimate reality, and insofar implicit witness thereto. Thus not only religion but all other forms of culture as well are forms of witness and, as such, part of the data on which theology in general is the critical reflection. Religion, however, being *explicit* witness to God or ultimate reality, may be said to provide the *privileged* data on which theology has the task of critically reflecting.

If this is how theology in general is to be understood, there remains an important difference between theology in general in the sense of *philosophical* theology, on the one hand, and theology in general in what I call the *generic/specific* sense, on the other. Theology in general in the sense of philosophical theology could, and presumably would, exist even in the absence of any specific religion or religions, provided only that something was at least implicitly thought, said, or done about God or ultimate reality and someone was able and willing to ask critically about its meaning and the validity of the claims that it expressed or implied. But theology in general in the generic/specific sense neither would nor could exist except as the theology corresponding to some specific religion. So, if religion, as was said, provides the privileged data for theology in general in both senses of the term, the data peculiar to some specific religion provide the *twice-privileged* data for theology in the generic/specific sense.

In the nature of the case, theology in general, whether philosophical theology or theology in the generic/specific sense corresponding to some specific religion or form of witness, can be done only in and for some particular historical situation, and given its particular problems and its resources for solving them. Consequently, there cannot be any such thing as *the* theology, unless, perhaps, as my teacher, Rudolf Bultmann liked to say, as an "eschatological phenomenon." The theological conversation is always both unconcluded and inconclusive, requiring to be taken up ever again afresh and *ab ovo*—yes, from the egg!—in each new situation. And this is so, even if one certainly can and should learn as much as possible

3

from all previous phases of the conversation about how one may best go about continuing it in one's own time and place.

Finally, the service that theology in general is in a position to perform for the witness on which it is the critical reflection is, in the nature of the case, an *indirect* service only. Like any other form of critical reflection, theology must remain free not only to *validate* the claims to validity that witness makes or implies, but also, as the case may be, to *invalidate* them. But, then, its only service to witness has to be indirect, any direct service being really no service at all—as critical reflection.

1.2. CHRISTIAN THEOLOGY IN PARTICULAR

If theology in general may be defined as critical appropriation of witness in general, including the implicit witness of secular culture as well as the explicit witness of religion, Christian theology in particular may be defined as *critical appropriation of specifically Christian witness*, including the implicit witness of Christian culture as well as the explicit witness of the Christian religion. This implies, of course, that one could offer an analogous definition of the form of critical reflection corresponding respectively to any other particular religion or form of witness. Thus the distinctive feature of Christian theology in particular, just as, analogously, of any other particular theology, is that its twice-privileged data are those provided by the witness of faith made explicit by the Christian religion.

Before proceeding, I recall the point made in passing in the previous section that the critical reflection proper to theology in general and therefore also to Christian theology in particular includes two things: critical *interpretation* of the meaning of witness—in the case of Christian theology, the meaning of Christian witness—and critical *validation* of the claims to validity that witness as such—or Christian witness as such—makes or implies. To say anything further, then, about Christian theology in particular requires asking about the claims to validity that Christian witness does make or imply. Anything like a complete answer to this question would require considering all of the different kinds of claims to validity that Christian witness makes or implies in common with all other religions or forms of witness and, indeed, with all of the other speech acts that human beings typically perform in thinking, saying, and doing whatever they think, say, and do. But I will focus here solely on the more or less distinctive claims that Christian witness makes or implies simply as such—simply as and because it is specifically *Christian* witness.

These claims, on my analysis, are the two claims that reflect the twofold structure of Christian witness itself as well as the systematic ambiguity of the term "witness," by which we can mean either the *act* of witnessing or the *content* of witness. Corresponding to this duality, any instance of Christian witness makes or implies two claims to validity: (1) that, as an explication or implication of the content of Christian witness, it is *adequate* to this content; and (2) that, as an act of Christian witness performed in and for a particular situation, it is *fitting* to this situation. The first claim itself, however, proves upon reflection to involve two further claims: that what is expressed or implied by the witness is *appropriate* to Jesus Christ because it is in agreement with what we may call the formally normative Christian witness attested by scripture and the rest of Christian tradition; and that what is expressed or implied by the witness is *credible* to human existence because it is in agreement with the truth about existence attested more or less adequately by human culture and religion otherwise.

But if any instance of Christian witness involves making or implying these two, or, really, three claims—to be adequate and also fitting, and so both appropriate and credible—whether or not the claims are valid neither is nor ever can be settled simply by making or implying them. On the contrary, all such claims are in principle problematic, and become problematic in fact as soon as they are called into question by the same claims' being made for a more or less different, or contrary, instance of Christian witness, or for some other non-Christian witness to the meaning of ultimate reality for us, either already borne or now in prospect. Thus whether any witness is as fitting or as adequate, and thus as appropriate or as credible, as it at least implicitly claims to be is always open to question; and Christian theology in particular is either the process or the product of the critical reflection—the critical interpretation and the critical validation—whereby this question can alone be pursued in a more or less deliberate, methodical, and reasoned way.

On my analysis, it is the distinctive task of Christian *practical theology* to validate the claim of Christian witness to be fitting to its situation, while it is the distinctive task of Christian *systematic theology* to validate the other claim of Christian witness to be adequate to its content, and so both appropriate to Jesus Christ and credible to human existence. Our special concern here, obviously, is with Christian systematic theology— together with the other disciplines and fields of inquiry that are involved, in one way or another, in carrying out its task. One such discipline is the third discipline of specifically Christian theology itself—namely, Christian *historical* (including *biblical*) *theology*, whose work is indispensable to systematic theology in its critically validating the claim of witness to be appropriate to Jesus Christ because it is in agreement with the formally normative Christian witness attested by scripture and tradition. But systematic theology also has to rely on the work of secular history generally, even as it must also depend on the independent discipline of philosophical theology, as well as on the field of philosophy as a whole, especially in its efforts to critically validate the other claim of Christian witness to be credible to human existence because it is in agreement with the truth about human existence originally disclosed by common human experience and reason.

Beyond this, I would call attention briefly to two points: (1) that, for all of their differences, the three disciplines of Christian theology—historical, systematic, and practical—are simply interrelated moments in the one complex movement of critical reflection required to validate the claims of Christian witness to be adequate to its content and fitting to its situation; and (2) that, for all of its necessary dependence on such other disciplines and fields as history and philosophy, and, in the case of practical theology, also on the human sciences and the various arts, Christian theology is nonetheless a distinctive form of critical reflection irreducible to any other.

As with theology in general, Christian theology in particular, including systematic theology, is always done in and for a particular situation, in terms of its particular problems and its resources for solving them. This means, among other things, that, although the *criteria* of theological judgment—i.e., adequacy, and so appropriateness and credibility, and also fittingness—are situation-*invariant* and therefore always the same from one historical situation to another, the *specific requirements* of these criteria are situation-*dependent* and therefore always more or less different in one situation than in another. What is appropriate or credible in this situation is not so in that, and what may be fitting here may not be fitting there.

Also true of Christian theology in particular, even as of theology in general, is that its service to Christian witness can never be more than indirect. Just as, in general, there can be critical reflection only where there is the possibility of invalidating claims as well as validating them, so in the particular case of Christian theology the theologian has to be free not only to validate the claims of Christian witness to be adequate to its content and fitting to its situation, but also to invalidate them. Here, too, there is a difference in principle between *making or implying claims* to validity, as one necessarily does in performing the act of Christian witness, and *critically reflecting* on such claims, as one does insofar as one engages in Christian theology. But this, unfortunately, is anything but a noncontroversial point. Again and again, from ancient times right up to the present, the roles of bearing witness and doing theology by critically reflecting on witness have been confused, with the unhappy result that any enforcement of doctrinal discipline has appeared to undercut any exercise of theological freedom—and vice versa. On the view presented here, by contrast, the relation between Christian witness and Christian theology is genuinely dialectical, in that they are distinct and never to be confused, and yet also related and never to be separated. But this means that, although Christian theology's proper service to Christian witness is real, it can never be more than indirect.

Ordinarily, a Christian's being a professional theologian is a particular Christian vocation, on all fours with a Christian's being an engineer or a doctor, a business person or a homemaker. But being a *professional* theologian is one thing, being a *lay* theologian, something else—just as the same is true of being a professional minister and being a lay minister. Even as each Christian is called to bear witness and thus to be a lay minister, regardless of her or his particular vocation or profession, so each Christian is also called to be a lay theologian, in order to, or for the sake of, her or his Christian witness and ministry.

1.3. CHRISTIAN SYSTEMATIC THEOLOGY

1.3.0. Two Inescapable Tasks

Since our concern here is with doing systematic theology, I shall focus attention henceforth on it. Given the understanding of systematic theology already clarified, there are evidently two inescapable tasks encompassed by its one task as a theological discipline. This one task, it will be recalled, is to validate critically the claim of Christian witness to be adequate to its content. Therefore, the first task that must be undertaken, which I distinguish as systematic theology's "dogmatic" task, is to validate critically the claim of Christian witness to be appropriate to Jesus Christ, while

1/3

7

the second task, which I call its "apologetic" task, is to validate critically the claim of Christian witness to be credible to human existence. I think and speak of the dogmatic task as first, relative to the second apologetic task, because, unless an instance of witness is appropriate to Jesus Christ, it cannot be valid *Christian* witness even if it should prove to be credible to human existence. By somewhat similar reasoning, I hold systematic theology to be logically prior to practical theology; for even if an instance of witness should prove to be fitting to its situation, it cannot be valid *Christian* witness unless it is adequate to its content and therefore both appropriate to Jesus Christ and credible to human existence. Still, the dogmatic task of systematic theology cannot be its only task, since it is also always faced with the apologetic task of validating the claim of witness to be credible to human existence, practically as well as theoretically.

But if these are the two main tasks of systematic theology, and thus what there is for it to do, how, more exactly, is it to be done? How is systematic theology supposed to accomplish its two tasks as a theological discipline? This is the question of the *method* of systematic theology—or, better, of its *methods*; for just as its task is not single but multiple, so, too, is its method. You may say, if you will, that the method of systematic theology is a method-encompassing-method, even as its task is a task-encompassing-task. Specifically, its method encompasses *three* main methods, corresponding to the three main phases in the single process of critical reflection by which it performs the two successive validations that it has the task of performing. None of the three methods it encompasses is peculiarly "theological," but rather is otherwise followed in human reflection generally, in one or more of the so-called secular, nontheological fields or disciplines. What makes any of these methods theological, insofar as it is so, is simply the encompassing method of theological reflection of which it is a part and, in particular, the distinctive claims to validity that following it is needed to validate. Naturally, each of the three methods specific to one or the other of the three phases may itself be complex, in that it in turn encompasses still more specific methods, and so on. It is not necessary for our purposes, however, to pursue our question into such detail. So I shall consider simply the three methods specific to the three main phases of systematic theological reflection without going into the complexity that each of them may in turn involve.

1.3.1. *The Historical Phase*

The first phase of systematic theology is its *historical* phase, and the method specific to it, historical method. In this phase, the objective of theological reflection is to meet the first of the two conditions that are necessary to validating critically the claim of witness to be appropriate to Jesus Christ. To validate this claim, theology must first determine both in principle and in fact what is to count as formally normative witness.

By "*normative* witness" I mean any witness that, being itself appropriate, properly functions as a norm for validating the appropriateness of some or all other witnesses. If the witness in question properly functions to validate *some* other witnesses, I speak of it as "*substantially* normative," because it thereby agrees in substance with all other appropriate witnesses. If, however, the witness in question properly functions to validate the appropriateness of *all* other witnesses, I distinguish it as also "*formally* normative," because it is the one witness with which *any* other has to agree in substance in order to be appropriate. Theology's first objective, then, is to identify what properly functions in this sense as formally normative witness, and to do this in fact as well as in principle. But this it can do only by determining the conditions that any witness must satisfy in order to function properly as formally normative and by then identifying the particular witness that satisfies (or the particular witnesses that satisfy) these necessary conditions.

The main method systematic theology must follow in order to do this can only be historical method. For what is to count as formally normative witness both in principle and in fact is what witness itself asserts or implies to be so; and this, like witness, is given only through particular historical experience and can therefore be determined only by following a properly historical method of critical reflection. This explains why, in its first phase, in which it has to follow such a method, systematic theology properly relies not only on its sister theological discipline, historical (including biblical) theology, but also on the secular field of history and its several disciplines.

The specific task of historical theology, which it carries out in continuous conversation with secular history, is to identify and understand the whole history of Christian witness, beginning with the earliest traditions lying behind, and now accessible only through, the writings of the New Testament. In performing this task, historical theology naturally comes to understand, among other things, what has in fact counted as formally normative witness in all the situations now past in which one witness or another has been borne. But it is just this that systematic theology evidently has to know in order to perform its specific tasks by first determining what is to count as formally normative witness. There is every reason, therefore, why the systematic theologian should learn as much as possible from all who do historical theology, including biblical theologians, as well as from secular historians. This does not mean, of course, that any of these fellow inquirers can be expected to do the systematic theologian's job or that she or he is obliged to accept the results of their inquiries without criticism. Although what witness is to count as formally normative can be determined only by historical inquiry, determining it is no part of any historical theologian's job, much less that of a secular historian. This remains an inalienable responsibility of the systematic theologian, and in discharging it she or he may by all means be critical of the results achieved by historical theologians and other historians, provided only that the grounds for any criticism are themselves results of properly historical inquiry.

But if how systematic theology is to proceed in this first phase is clear enough, how it is actually to be done is anything but easy, especially today. This is because there is less consensus now in Christian witness and theology even than in the past about what is to count as formally normative, either in principle or in fact. To be sure, from at least the second century, there has been widespread agreement about the basic principle: that witness is to count as formally normative which is *apostolic*, in the sense of being the original and originating and, therefore, constitutive witness of the church. But, aside from the fact, evidenced by the history of the canon, that there has always been disagreement about just what witness or witnesses can be validated as apostolic, exactly what the principle of apostolicity itself is to mean has been profoundly controversial. Thus, while Protestants, Roman Catholics, and Orthodox have all classically accepted the same apostolic principle, they have understood it in sharply different ways—Protestants appealing to "scripture alone" as apostolic, Roman Catholics and Orthodox invoking alternative understandings of "scripture and tradition" as the real meaning of apostolicity. And as if this were not enough, the revisionary forms of Christian witness and theology that have emerged in the course of modern church history—in so-called liberal Christianity, Roman Catholic as well as Protestant—have challenged the very principle of apostolicity, replacing it with an appeal to "the historical Jesus" as the real principle of formally normative witness.

There is little question, then, that any determination a theologian today can make of what is to count as formally normative witness will be even more controversial than ever before. The range of options has never been as great; and none of them is free enough from objections to make it the only reasonable choice. This does not imply, in my judgment, that no option is sufficiently better than all of the others to be at least relatively preferable. But it certainly does mean that critically validating the appropriateness of witness today can never be easy, and that doing systematic theology responsibly requires one to reckon with its difficulties.

As for my own option, it is distinctively different from both the classical and the revisionary positions to which I have just alluded. My contention is that what has been classically appealed to, in one way or another, as normative Christian witness—namely, scripture and tradition—can no longer be validly so appealed to. I am well aware that this is a highly controversial contention, and I cannot possibly argue for it here as I have elsewhere.[1] But notwithstanding the all but universal belief and practice to the contrary, one of the surest implications of historical-critical study of the Christian past is that the usual distinction between scripture and tradition completely breaks down—for the very good reason that scripture, so-called, or, more exactly, the part of scripture comprising the New Testament canon, must itself be said to be precisely "tradition" by the very principle or criterion historically used to set it apart from tradition. That criterion, as I have said, was "apostolicity," in the sense of the unique characteristic defining the witness of the apostles as the original and originating and, therefore, constitutive Christians—"disciples at first hand," in Søren Kierkegaard's phrase, as distinct from all other Christians who can only be "disciples at second hand." So, by this criterion, to be validly included on the list, or "canon," of writings comprising the New Testament required that a particular writing be deemed "apostolic" because authored by one of the apostles. But the ongoing course of historical-critical study of the New Testament writings, including especially what are called "source criticism" and "form criticism," has established beyond serious question that not one of the New Testament writings qualifies as "apostolic" by that criterion. Why not? Well, because they have all been shown to have been authored

---

1. See, e.g., Ogden, *Point of Christology*, 96–105; and Ogden, *On Theology*, 45–68.

by someone who, in her or his writing, made use of as sources, oral and/ or written, other Christian witness or witnesses earlier than itself—from which the obvious inference is that it itself could not possibly be formally "apostolic" in the sense of being the earliest, original and originating, and therefore constitutive Christian witness.

But if this inference effectively undermines all of the classical positions on the norms of Christian witness—whether Protestant, Roman Catholic, or Orthodox—yet another result of the same ongoing historical-critical study is that the alternative position typically held by modern revisionary Christians and theologians is likewise indefensible. I refer to the position according to which the real norm is not the witness of the apostles and all subsequent witness substantially agreeing with it—in other words, scripture and tradition—but rather the witness of Jesus himself, the so-called historical Jesus, as he actually was prior to any and all interpretations of him by others. The insurmountable difficulty with this revisionary position is that there simply are not any primary sources for Jesus's own witness—no sayings from his own mouth, no writings from his own hand, and so on. Even our earliest sources—those that can be reconstructed by working back from the synoptic gospels, on the one hand, and the writings of Paul, on the other—are at best secondary, and are one and all witnesses of faith, not historical reports in our usual modern sense of the term. Consequently, although we can indeed distinguish *theoretically* between the earliest Christian witness to Jesus and Jesus's own witness, we are quite unable to distinguish them *operationally*, so as to identify in a non-question-begging way what Jesus himself said and did prior to any and all interpretations of him by others—the others who responded to his call with obedient faith and then bore witness, in their several ways, to his decisive significance for human existence. Thus, contrary to the reiterated claims of all those best known in our own country through the work of "the Jesus Seminar," any quest of the historical Jesus, old, new, or renewed, is really quite impossible. The only possibility allowed for by the very nature of our only sources is something quite different: not a quest of the historical Jesus, but, as Willi Marxsen distinguishes it, a historical quest for Jesus, whose only attainable objective is the Jesus attested by the earliest Christian witness now accessible to us.[2]

2. See, e.g., Marxsen, *Jesus and Easter*, 21–23.

My own position on formally normative witness, then, is a third, or mean, position between the usual two extremes. On the one hand, it agrees with the classical position in accepting the principle or criterion of apostolicity as against the revisionary appeal to the historical Jesus. On the other hand, it insists that the only witness that can now be validated in fact by this apostolic principle is not, as the classical position holds, the canon of the New Testament, but rather a canon *before* this canon, although not the witness of the historical Jesus, as the revisionary position holds, but rather the earliest Christian witness or witnesses to Jesus that we are now able to reconstruct, employing our own historical-critical methods and knowledge.

As preferable as I take this position to be to its alternatives, however, it is not without problems of its own. So I repeat my statement that critically validating the appropriateness of witness today can never be easy, and that doing systematic theology responsibly requires one to recognize this.

1.3.2. *The Hermeneutical Phase*

Much the same can be said about the second, *hermeneutical* phase of systematic theology, where it follows a specifically hermeneutical method. Here there are two objectives of theological reflection, even though both are accomplished by doing one and the same thing. The one objective is to meet the second of the two conditions that are necessary to critically validating the claim of witness to be appropriate to Jesus Christ. To validate this claim, theology not only has to determine what witness is to count as formally normative, in fact as well as in principle, but must also understand, and therefore interpret, this witness so that it can actually perform its proper function as formal norm. But the interpretation of the norm that is thus required to validate the appropriateness of witness is exactly what is also required to accomplish the other objective of theological reflection in its second phase—namely, to meet the first of the two conditions that are necessary to validating the claim of witness to be credible to human existence. Before the credibility of witness can be validated as the truth about human existence, what witness does and does not mean to say concerning this truth has to be understood, and this, too, requires interpretation of formally normative witness.

The method that such interpretation calls for is what I mean by "hermeneutical method"—and, as I should perhaps add, all that I mean by it, for the purposes of the present argument. The method in question might also be called "exegetical method," although, by either name, it is the procedure one has to follow in order to understand and interpret formally normative witness in relation to the kind of human question to which it itself is addressed as an answer. Assuming, as I do—for reasons that will gradually become clearer as I develop my argument—that the question properly addressed by witness, beginning with formally normative witness, is the existential question about the meaning of ultimate reality for us, we may say that the proper hermeneutical method for theology is what has been called, by Bultmann and others, "existentialist interpretation." Whether we call it this or not, however, if witness itself is addressed to the existential question, it must be understood and interpreted accordingly; and this means that it must be interpreted in concepts and terms in which this question today can be rightly asked and answered and human existence itself rightly thought and spoken about. This is the reason why, in this second hermeneutical phase, in which systematic theology must work out just such an interpretation, it properly looks for help not only to historical theology and secular history, but also to the secular field of philosophy and to its discipline of philosophical theology in particular.

That systematic theology should rely here, too, on historical theology and, indirectly, on secular history will be obvious. As understanding of the whole history of Christian witness, historical theology and, in particular, biblical theology, includes understanding of formally normative witness as well. But because understanding witness also requires interpreting it, historical theology itself is and must be already dependent on philosophy and philosophical theology. This is so because to interpret what is thought and spoken in one set of concepts and terms always requires another set into which to interpret it. And it is precisely the business of philosophy and, in the case of the existential question addressed by witness, of philosophical theology to provide the requisite set of concepts and terms. Consequently, systematic theologians have every reason to learn whatever they can not only from historical theologians and secular historians, but also from all who do secular philosophy in general and philosophical theology in particular. Again, this does not imply that the systematic theologian can alienate her or his own responsibility either to historians or to philosophers or that she or he must accept uncritically whatever they happen to say. Interpretation of the witness that is to count as formally normative as precisely that remains the systematic theologian's responsibility. And this means that she or he is also responsible for criticizing the work of philosophers as well as historians, provided only that the method followed in doing so is the same hermeneutical method that they in their ways must play a role in developing.

But, as I have already indicated, how systematic theology is actually to be done in this second phase is also problematic, especially for anyone doing it today. In this phase, the source of the difficulties is the extensive plurality of both theologies and philosophies, which has continued only to grow with the passage of time. Clearly, from the earliest beginnings of the church, there has never been simply one Christian witness, but only many Christian witnesses, through which Christians have expressed their experience of Jesus and asserted his decisive significance. But this plurality at the primary level of self-understanding and life-praxis is scarcely reduced, if it is reduced at all, at the secondary level of critical reflection, where there has never been simply one interpretation of formally normative witness, but only many. A principal reason for this, of course, is that there have also always been many philosophies, in the sense of secular interpretations of human culture and religion generally. Depending on which of these many philosophies have provided their concepts and terms, there have also been many theologies. This means that new philosophies that have continued to be developed have allowed for yet other theological interpretations beyond those already represented by traditional theologies.

The upshot of this is that no interpretation of formally normative witness today can expect to surmount this ever-growing plurality of other theologies and philosophies. At best, it will be but one interpretation among many; and if this need not preclude its being at least relatively more appropriate than other interpretations, the odds against its actually being so have never been greater,

1.3.3. *The Philosophical Phase*

This brings us to the third and last phase of systematic theology, which is its *philosophical* phase, where the method specific to it is philosophical method. In this phase, the objective of theological reflection is to meet the second condition that is necessary to validating critically the claim of witness to be credible to human existence. To validate this claim, theology not only must interpret the witness that is to count as formally normative, but also has to determine what is to count as the truth about human existence both in principle and in fact. Here, again, I am simply assuming that the human question to which Christian witness is addressed is the existential question about the meaning of ultimate reality for us. If this assumption is sound, the claim to credibility that witness makes or implies is a claim to *existential* credibility. It claims to be worthy of belief because it expresses truth, and the truth it expresses is existential truth. But, then, to validate this claim, systematic theology has to determine what is to count as such truth, and this in fact as well as in principle. And this it can do only by determining the criteria that any assertion must satisfy to be existentially true and then formulating an understanding of ultimate reality that satisfies these criteria, which means, of course, satisfying the specific requirements of the criteria in the given historical situation.

The method required to do this evidently has to be philosophical method. For what is to count as existential truth both in principle and in fact is what human existence itself discloses to be so; and this, like existence, is given only through common human experience and can therefore be determined only by following a properly philosophical method of reflection. Because this is so, theology in its third phase, in which it must follow such a method, also properly relies on any assistance it can get from the secular field of philosophy and its particular discipline, philosophical theology.

I already indicated that, in my sense of the word, "philosophy" means, whatever else it may mean, the secular analysis and interpretation of human culture and religion generally. This is the reason, indeed, that theology properly looks for philosophy's help, and especially for philosophical theology's, in working out its own interpretation of Christian witness in particular. But if philosophy, too, has a hermeneutical phase, the objective in its final phase, or, at any rate, in the final phase of philosophical theology, is a reflective understanding of the truth about human existence, and thus of the criteria proper for critically validating all formulations of this truth. Just such an understanding, however, is what theology clearly has to have in order to carry out its specific tasks by finally determining what is to count as existential truth. Therefore, in this third phase, also, systematic theologians have the best of reasons for learning everything they can from secular philosophers and philosophical theologians. Once again, this in no way implies either that they can leave their job to these others or that they must accept without question whatever the others happen to come up with. They remain fully responsible for validating the credibility of Christian witness; and in exercising this responsibility, they not only may but also must ask questions about the others' claims to existential truth, provided only that their reasons for doing so arise out of their own pursuit of a properly philosophical method of reflection.

In this phase, too, however, how systematic theology is actually to be done involves serious difficulties, especially for anyone attempting to do it today. The main reason for this, of course, is the same ever-growing plurality of theologies and philosophies as well as of religions and cultures already referred to. Not only have human beings always had many different and often conflicting understandings of existential truth, but they have also never been able to agree on the criteria proper for adjudicating their differences. In fact, some of the bitterest and most intractable human conflicts have arisen from irresolvable differences over just these criteria and their specific requirements in a given situation. Nor has the extent of such plurality at the primary level of self-understanding and life-praxis ever been significantly reduced at the secondary level of critical reflection and proper theory. There, also, the one truth about human existence has been present only in the many *claims* to truth, not all of which can possibly be valid.

But if this has always been the case in any situation in which theology could have been done, it is still more strikingly the case in our situation today. With the emergence for the first time in history of a truly global human community, the plurality of claims to truth with which theology somehow has to reckon has become practically limitless. It now comprises not only all the classical expressions of world cultures and religions, but also all the more or less radical revisions of these expressions, including the modern secularistic humanisms, both evolutionary and revolutionary. And of particular importance for theology are the significant challenges to traditional understandings of truth that are now coming from groups and individuals hitherto marginalized and unheard from for reasons of class, race, gender, or ethnicity. These challenges converge in insisting with new urgency that the truth about existence is not only to be believed but also done and that therefore any claim to tell it must be credible practically as well as theoretically.

The import of all this is that Christian systematic theology today has an all but impossible job in determining what is to count as the truth about human existence. My own belief is that the job can still be done, or, at any rate, reasonably attempted, insofar as some understandings of this truth are at least relatively more credible than others. But if there was ever a time when systematic theologians could have been excused for looking solely to some one theology or philosophy to provide such an understanding, it has long since passed. We today are without excuse for all of our traditional provincialisms, and we must scrupulously avoid even a hint of dogmatism in our attempts to formulate existential truth.

This, then, is my answer to the question of the method, or methods, of Christian systematic theology, and thus of how we are to do it today. There are certain dangers, admittedly, in distinguishing, as I have, between its three different phases, insofar as they may be falsely separated or their priority relative to each other construed too simply. Even so, the three phases, like their methods, are as distinct as they are inseparable, and their order is preserved even though it is evident that the first in a way implies the third as well as the second, even as the second in a way implies the third as well as the first.

1.4. SUMMARY AND CONCLUSION

I shall now briefly review the main points I have tried to make on prolegomena, and then make one final point.

First of all, I have proceeded throughout on the basis of a fundamental distinction between, on the one hand, making or implying claims to validity, as we necessarily do in understanding ourselves and leading our lives, and, on the other hand, critically reflecting on our self-understanding and life-praxis so as to interpret their meaning and with a view to validating (or, as the case may be, invalidating) our claims. I applied this distinction, first, in defining theology in general—namely, by distinguishing theology, properly so-called, from witness, understanding the term "witness" to refer to everything that we think, say, and do about God or ultimate reality except for such thought and/or speech as are involved in critically appropriating all this, to which the term "theology" properly refers.

Christian theology in particular, then, I defined accordingly as the thought and/or speech involved in critically reflecting on the meaning of specifically Christian witness and its distinctive claims to validity. These claims, I argued, are the two claims that the witness in question is adequate to its content, and therefore both appropriate to Jesus Christ and credible to human existence, and that the witness is fitting to its situation. Assigning critical validation of the second claim to practical theology, I took validation of the first claim, and thus successive validations of the two claims that it in turn encompasses, to be the proper task or tasks of systematic theology.

In the third section of the chapter, then, I argued that there are three distinct phases to the single movement of reflection whereby Christian systematic theology carries out these two successive validations and that there is a correspondingly distinct method specific to each of these phases. Thus I tried to show that and why the method of systematic theology in its first phase is historical, in its second phase, hermeneutical, and in its third phase, philosophical. Withal, I tried to explain why systematic theology can accomplish its task only by surmounting the difficulties attending each of these three phases—especially the formidable historical difficulties of determining what is to count both in principle and in fact as formally normative witness and the certainly not less formidable philosophical difficulties of determining what is to count both in principle and in fact as the truth about human existence.

This brings me to a final point. Considering the difficulties of accomplishing systematic theology's task, we should not be surprised that so few are willing to undertake it without trying, in one way or another, to evade it or to make it appear easier than it is. Perhaps none of us would be up to it if we really took its measure and dismissed the reassurances that so many are eager to give us that the task is, after all, easy. In any case, it would be altogether impossible for any of us if we allowed ourselves to suppose that we could never responsibly come to any conclusions until we had first considered all of the relevant data and arguments, historical, hermeneutical, and philosophical.

But the mark of a rational conclusion is not that such exhaustive consideration already lies behind it, but that it ever remains open to correction pending any such exhaustive consideration and that it facilitates completely open and unrestricted criticism with a view to being thus corrected. One way of facilitating such criticism is to take pains to say what one means, and to mean what one says, explicitly delimiting one's conclusions in proportion to the evidence available to support them, argumentative as well as experiential. More important still is working hard to take the full measure of the problems one is up against and to identify all the options for possibly solving them between which one may be reasonably expected to choose.

In short, the real test of one's rationality as a human being, and of one's good faith as a theologian, is not so much what one does *before* reaching one's conclusions as what one does *after* reaching them. Recognizing this, any of us can take up the task and do as much as we can to accomplish it, never forgetting that the systematic theological conversation of which we thereby become a part is not only always unconcluded but also always inconclusive. And all who undertake the task as a Christian vocation may also ever remind themselves that, in this, as in everything else they do, they neither are nor can be justified by their own good works, but are and must be justified solely by God's grace, through faith alone.

2

On God

2.0. PRELIMINARY REMARKS

CHRISTIAN SYSTEMATIC THEOLOGY, I have argued, is critical reflection on Christian witness with a view to validating its claim to be adequate to its content because it is both appropriate to Jesus Christ and credible to human existence. It is appropriate to Jesus Christ, if it is, because it is in substantial agreement with the formally normative witness of the apostles attested by scripture and the rest of Christian tradition; and it is credible to human existence, if it is, because it both confirms and is confirmed by the truth about existence attested more or less adequately by all human culture and religion.

But just what is Christian witness? Considering the starting point of our reflections, in the definition of "theology" suggested by the literal meaning of the word as thought and/or speech about God, we could say that Christian witness is the thought and/or speech about God that arises from specifically Christian experience and faith. But, then, what is specifically Christian experience and faith if not the experience of Jesus and the faith in God that is mediated decisively through him insofar as one is either an apostle or else someone who experiences Jesus and believes in God *with* the apostles, in communion with them? By "apostles" here, I should perhaps explain again, I mean those who were the first so to experience Jesus as to come to this faith in God through him, and whose witness of faith, being the original and originating, and hence constitutive Christian witness, is, accordingly, formally normative.

The interesting thing about Christian witness, however, is that its constitutive assertion—the assertion that constitutes it explicitly as such, that makes it *Christian* witness—is really two assertions. It is not simply an assertion about God, but also an assertion about Jesus Christ. It is *logos* about *christos* as well as *logos* about *theos*, christology as well as theology. Nevertheless, the first thing to be considered now, in this presentation, even as in most of the classic formulations of Christian faith in both creeds and theologies, is not Jesus Christ but God. How does one account for this? Why, if one is a Christian, does one's theology properly begin with God rather than with Jesus Christ? Or does it?

I believe it does—not, however, because any theology can be other than thoroughly christocentric and still be an appropriate Christian theology. On the contrary, theology properly begins with God, not *in spite* of the constitutive christological assertion, but precisely *because* of it. I say this for two reasons.

First of all, because, as I have said, Christian witness is constituted explicitly as such, not merely by one, but by two assertions: by the theological assertion about God as well as by the christological assertion about Jesus. But I say it, secondly, because, when the christological assertion itself is understood as it should be, in relation to the question it is intended to answer, it is not only, or primarily, an assertion about Jesus; it is also, and above all, an assertion about God—about who God is and, precisely thereby, about who each of us is and is authorized to be in relation to God. In other words, a certain understanding of who God is, or, better, of what strictly ultimate reality is, in its meaning for us, is not only the most important implication of the christological assertion but also its most fundamental presupposition.

This is clear, I believe, from an analysis of the predicate term of the christological assertion and of how this term actually functions in it. In the classical formulation of the assertion, "Jesus is the Christ," this term is "the Christ," which, as is well known, derives from the Greek translation of the Aramaic term "Messiah," meaning "the anointed one," and, specifically, the one who, according to certain late Jewish eschatological expectations, is to rule as God's vicegerent in the last days. But this implies, naturally, that it would make no sense to say that Jesus (or anyone else) is the Christ unless there were a God and unless this God had a meaning for us that Jesus (or someone else) could be said to re-present in a decisive way. This is why I say that a certain understanding of who God is, and thus of what strictly ultimate reality is, is the most fundamental *presupposition* of the christological assertion itself, in this or any other formulation. But if we ask just how the predicate term "the Christ" functions in this formulation, it is clear that, while it certainly functions to *interpret* the subject of whom it is predicated, and thus to tell us who Jesus is—namely, that he is the chosen one of God through whom the meaning of God for us is decisively re-presented—it also functions in such a way as to *be interpreted by* this selfsame subject, Jesus, so that we are told at one and the same time who the Christ is, and, therefore, who God is, and who, accordingly, we ourselves also are and are to be.

Consequently, I say that a certain understanding of who God is, is also the most important *implication* of the christological assertion. It is its most important implication, because it is precisely the question about who God is, or about what strictly ultimate reality is, in its meaning for us, that is our most important question as human beings, solely and simply because we are human, because we share in the universal reality of humanness.

2.1. THE QUESTION ABOUT GOD

The main thesis I shall now explain and argue for is that the question about God is a special form of the more general question about ultimate reality and, more exactly, about strictly ultimate reality. By the term "reality" in general, I mean, in William James's words, "what we in some way find ourselves obliged to take account of."[1] Accepting this definition, we may infer that "*ultimate* reality" covers everything that we are all finally obliged to take account of insofar as we exist humanly at all, whatever other things we may or may not have to take account of in each leading our own individual lives, all of which we may distinguish as comprising "*immediate* reality." In this sense, ultimate reality includes everything necessary in our experience or self-understanding, as distinct from all the other things that we may or may not experience and understand because they are merely contingent relative to our own existence simply as such. So, whatever else it includes, ultimate reality includes our own existence as selves, together with everything that is in any way a necessary condition of the possibility of our existence, whether other human selves or the still larger world of subhuman and possibly even superhuman beings, along with whatever they in turn all necessarily imply. Among the conditions that are thus necessary, obviously, is any reality that can be said to be "*strictly* ultimate," because it is a necessary condition of the possibility not only of *human* existence, but also of *any* existence whatever. Thus strictly

1. James, *Some Problems of Philosophy*, 101.

ultimate reality is what not only we, but any being that is so much as possible, is obliged somehow to take account of, if only in the completely general way of being really, internally related to it and therefore dependent on it and affected by it.

But now we can ask about ultimate reality, including strictly ultimate reality, in two clearly different, if nonetheless closely related, ways. We can ask about it more *concretely* or existentially, insofar as we ask about *its meaning for us* and therefore ask, at one and the same time, about both it and about how we are to understand ourselves and conduct our lives in relation to it. Or we can ask about it more *abstractly* or intellectually, insofar as we prescind from ourselves and our relation to it and ask only about it, in *its structure in itself*. The more concrete or existential way of asking our question necessarily includes, or implies, the more abstract or intellectual way. For in asking about the meaning of ultimate reality for us, we are by implication asking about its structure in itself. But if the existential way of asking the question thus has intellectual—and, more exactly, *metaphysical*—implications, it has *moral* implications as well. Why? Because in asking how we are to understand ourselves in relation to ultimate reality, we are also asking—in part, directly, and in part, by implication—how we ourselves are to act and what we are to do. On my analysis, then, the existential question about ultimate reality has these two aspects, metaphysical and moral, in which it is at once closely related to, and yet distinct from, the properly metaphysical question, on the one hand, and the properly moral question, on the other.

If we ask, then: What makes our asking the existential question about ultimate reality *possible*? my answer is: a basic faith in the meaning of life, or in the meaning for us of ultimate reality, including strictly ultimate reality. This means that, in asking our existential question, we do not ask *whether* ultimate reality has a meaning for us, and so authorizes us to understand ourselves in one way and not in another, but only *what* meaning it has for us, and thus *how* it authorizes us to understand ourselves and lead our lives.

But why is asking this existential question *necessary*? Here there seem to me to be at least two factors that need to be taken into account. First of all, the negativities of our existence as we actually live it—such things as guilt, suffering, solitariness, and death—all call into question the answers that we are accustomed to give to the question, mainly because of the way in which we have been brought up in our particular society and culture, including our particular religion. But, then, secondly, insofar as we become aware of the plurality of answers that have, in fact, been given to the question by different human groups and individuals, we are apt to find ourselves seeking *the* answer to it, in the sense of the *decisive* answer—the answer that, being *true*, answers our question and also enables us to decide responsibly with respect to all of the other answers.

My thesis is that the question about God to which the Christian witness, and so both assertions constituting that witness, christological as well as theological, give answer is a special form of this existential question about the meaning of ultimate reality for us. It is the form that this existential question takes, once a certain answer to it has already been given—namely, the answer given by what I call "radical monotheism," according to which *God* is strictly ultimate reality, which means, of course, conversely, that the strictly ultimate reality with which all of us somehow have to do is the One radical monotheists call "God."

At the risk of making an awfully complex story far too simple, let me put it this way: the concept "God," as conceived by radical monotheism, includes two aspects: on the one hand, God is the strictly ultimate reality that not only we, but also everything else that is so much as possible must somehow take account of; and on the other hand, God is the kind of reality that can and does take account of us, that is really, internally related to us, affected by us, even dependent on us—to which we, in some way, make a difference. In other words, God is not only a reality, indeed, *strictly ultimate* reality, God is also a *concrete* reality, more exactly, an *individual* reality, which, as such, may be more or less aptly symbolized in personal terms. Thus, for radical monotheism, God is understood as the one strictly universal individual, whose field of interaction with self and others is absolutely unrestricted, being action on and reaction to *all* things, possible as well as actual. Not only is it true that all things are really, internally related to God, but it is also true that the God to whom they are all related is really, internally related to all of them. In short: for radical monotheism, the truth that is ever in dispute in the open dialogue involving the vast plurality of claims to truth in different human situations is not only, or primarily, the God-relatedness of all things, but also, and above all, *the all things-relatedness of God.*

Once, however, strictly ultimate reality is conceived in this radically monotheistic way, the existential question about it, and thus about its meaning for us, takes the special form of *the question about God,* about what *God* means for us and, therefore, about how we are authorized to understand ourselves and everything else in relation to *God*.

2.2. GOD WHO GIVES US THE VICTORY THROUGH OUR LORD JESUS CHRIST

Up to this point, I have been trying to clarify and justify my claim that a certain understanding of God is the *most fundamental presupposition* of the Christian witness, being necessarily presupposed by both of the assertions explicitly constituting this witness, christological as well as theological. The question to which this witness gives an answer, I have argued, is not only, or primarily, the question, "Who is Jesus?" but also, and above all, the question, "Who is God?" which always means, of course, "What does God mean for us?" How are we to understand ourselves and lead our lives in relation to the strictly ultimate reality properly thought and spoken of as "God"? But, then, the most fundamental presupposition of asking this question is, as I have said, a certain understanding of God, of the strictly ultimate reality of our own existence *as* God, as *the God of radical monotheism*, the one universal individual, whose field of interaction is with all things and who, therefore, is at once their primal source and their final end—in Paul's language, the One "from whom are all things and for whom we exist" (1 Cor 8:6; cf. also Rom 11:36: the One "from whom and through whom and for whom are all things"). Unless this most basic presupposition of radical monotheism were valid, the question about God to which the Christian witness gives an answer could not even be asked.

But if some such understanding of God is the most fundamental presupposition of the Christian witness, its *most important implication*, also, is likewise a certain understanding of God, which is expressed or implied by both of the assertions explicitly constituting this witness. If Jesus is, indeed, the Christ, who the Christ is, is decisively re-presented through Jesus, and this can only mean that it is also through Jesus that who God Godself is, is decisively re-presented—i.e., *re*-presented, presented *again*, a *second* time, *explicitly*, being always already presented *once*, the *first* time, *implicitly*, in and with the existence of each and every human being as soon and as long as she or he is human at all. Thus, when we read in the Prologue of the Gospel of John, "No one has ever seen God; the only Son, who is in the bosom of the Father, he has made God known" (John 1:18), we meet with a claim that not only identifies Jesus as the only Son of God, but, at one and the same time, also identifies the only true God as none other than the Father of Jesus.

My task, consequently, in this and the following section of this chapter on God is to sketch out at least the outlines of the understanding of God that is thus necessarily implied by the Christian witness as its most important implication. It is most important because it is expressed or implied by *both* of the assertions constituting this witness and because it alone serves to answer our most important question as human beings, which is to say, our existential question about the meaning of ultimate reality for us, and—if we already think and speak of ultimate reality in terms of the radical monotheism that the Christian witness necessarily presupposes—our existential question about the meaning of *God* for us. In the rest of this second section, I shall try to carry out this task by speaking, in Paul's words, of the "God who gives us the victory through our Lord Jesus Christ." In sec. 2.3, then, I shall proceed to speak briefly about why and in what sense, if any, this God can and should be spoken of as the triune God—the three-in-one God: Father, Son, and Holy Spirit—of Christian tradition.

Obviously, if the Christian answer to the question about who God really is, is implied by who Jesus really is—and this, I have argued, is the point of the christological assertion—then answering the question about God Christianly depends upon determining who Jesus really is. Who, then, is the Jesus we call Christ, and who, accordingly, is the God who gives us the victory through him?

At this crucial point, I have no alternative but simply to assume the validity of an answer to the question of who Jesus is that I will not be able to argue for adequately until my later discussion of Jesus Christ. But pending such further discussion, allow me to make two very basic points: one having to do with who Jesus is *formally*, the other with who Jesus is *materially*.

If my answer is correct to the question of formally normative Christian witness, which I briefly discussed in considering prolegomena, then who Jesus is formally can only be who Jesus is represented as being in the witness of the apostles that alone is formally normative for all Christian witness and theology. This, of course, is the point of the apostolic principle, according to which Jesus and the apostles are interdependent and require to be defined in terms of one another. Who Jesus is goes to define who the apostles are, and, conversely, who the apostles are goes to define who Jesus is. Just as the apostles are the original and originating, and therefore constitutive, Christian witnesses, whose witness arises out of their immediate experience of Jesus himself and derives such authority as it has solely from him, so Jesus is the one to whom the apostles bear witness and whom all other Christians are able to experience only mediately, solely through the apostles' witness.

But to make this first point that Jesus formally is the one to whom the apostles bear witness is not to answer the question of who Jesus is materially, or insofar as it asks about his material identity. The question remains, "Who *is* the Jesus to whom the apostles bear witness as the Christ?" The second point I need to make, then—but for which I also cannot argue further here—I can perhaps best make simply by reminding my reader of the answer to this very question that Charles Wesley gives in the line from his well-known hymn, "Love Divine, All Loves Excelling": "Jesus, thou art all compassion, pure, unbounded love thou art." If I am right, this answer to the question of who Jesus is succinctly summarizes exactly who Jesus is represented as being materially in the apostolic witness. As I hope to show more fully in my later consideration of christology, Jesus is represented in the earliest Christian witness now accessible to us precisely as the one who in various ways—through what he said, did, and suffered—confronted the witnesses explicitly and decisively with the gift and demand of God's own love, thereby authorizing them to exist in obedient faith. By such faith, I mean, as I understand the witnesses themselves also to have meant, both unreserved trust in God's love for themselves and for all and unqualified loyalty to the cause of God's love, loving God and their neighbors as themselves, thereby so bearing their witness to Jesus and to the God who has sent him, that, through their witness, others, also, might come to exist in this same way.

Whether I am right in this understanding of what Jesus means materially is a question I want the reader to defer until after my discussion of christology. In the meantime, I ask that it be simply assumed that this is who the earliest witnesses assert Jesus to be in order then to think with me about what it implies for the Christian understanding of who God is. This implication, simply put, is that God, which is to say, that strictly ultimate reality which we think and speak of as God insofar as we are radical monotheists—that God in this sense is the all-compassion, the pure, unbounded love, whose gift and demand become explicit, indeed, are decisively re-presented, through Jesus. But now just how are we to understand this?

The first step toward an answer is to consider *the use of language* involved in thinking and saying that the strictly ultimate reality called "God" is love. "Love," on any account, is a term whose ordinary uses are all in the context of our personal or interpersonal relations, where we experience ourselves as both the subjects and the objects of love, as those who love others and who are loved by them, be these others persons like ourselves or other beings also capable somehow of giving and receiving love. But now if we apply this term to God, which is to say, to the strictly ultimate reality but for which there neither would nor could be anything at all, we obviously cannot be using it in this same ordinary sense. For God, so understood, cannot possibly be simply one more person among others in literally the same sense in which we can say this of any of our-selves as human persons. The same is true, of course, of much of the rest of our language about God, which is likewise not literal but symbolic. In fact, the more such language comes out of our primary religious experi-ence and understanding, as distinct from our secondary theological and philosophical reflection thereon, the more likely it is to be language that can only be symbolic rather than literal in meaning.

And yet not *all* of our language about God can be symbolic, lest none of it be able to be so. Unless at least *some* things can be said about God literally rather than symbolically, we could never know that what we sup-posedly say about God symbolically is something really said *about* God at all, as distinct from merely expressing our subjective feelings or deci-sions, or simply misusing language whose proper use is not only different from, but also incompatible with, using it to speak of God. Thus, if for one to love is, by the very meaning of the word, for one to love someone or something other than oneself as loving, and to be really, internally related to this other, so that the other makes a real difference to one, then to say even symbolically that God is love is to imply that it must be not merely symbolically but literally true both that there is someone or something other than God Godself as loving that is the object of God's love and that God is really, internally related to this other, which therefore makes a real difference to God. So, if strictly ultimate reality is not as literally individual as it is universal, or if there is not literally someone or something other than the universal individual as loving, or if the universal individual is not literally related to this other really, internally, so that the other makes a real difference to the universal individual, then the statement that "God is love" cannot be true even symbolically.

But exactly what all *is* literally implied by the symbolic statement that God is love—i.e., "all-compassion," "pure, unbounded love"? Being *compassion* or *love*, God has to be a concrete *individual* not only acting on, but also being acted on by, and therefore interacting with, others ("compassion" meaning literally "suffering with"). On the other hand, being *all* compassion, or *pure, unbounded* love, God has to be the one and only *universal* individual, whose field of interacting with others is utterly unrestricted. This implies, naturally, that nothing whatever that is so much as possible either is or could be outside God's love or merely alongside God, for God in God's very essence *is* love.

The same implication follows ineluctably from Jesus's summary of the law in the two commandments that we shall love the Lord our God with the whole of our being and that we shall love our neighbors as ourselves. Clearly, if it is God whom we are to love with all of our powers, God must be one individual distinct, even if also inseparable, from all others whose interests we can take account of and act to realize. At the same time, if *all* of our powers are to be exercised in our love for the one individual God, even while we are also to accept our neighbors as ourselves and to act so as to realize all of their interests as well, God must also be strictly universal and all-inclusive, in that there can be no interest either of ourselves or of any of our neighbors that is not somehow included in the interests of God.

But if God, to be all-compassion, pure, unbounded love, has to be the universal individual, the structure of God's being in itself has to be a genuinely *dipolar*, not a merely monopolar, structure. Not only must there be the relatively more *active* pole of God's *acting on* all others, but there must also be the relatively more *passive* pole of God's *being acted on by* all others, and thus suffering with them. This means that the radical uniqueness—and, in that sense, the "transcendence"—of God relative to all others can only be, as Charles Hartshorne rightly argues, a "*dual* transcendence." God is and must be in every respect unique, in some sense incomparable, because God is by definition the One "than whom," in Anselm of Canterbury's famous formula, "none greater can be conceived." But if the structure of God's being in itself has to be dipolar, God is unsurpassable and therefore unique and incomparable, not in one respect only, but in two. God is not only unsurpassably active, because acting on *all* others; God is also unsurpassably passive, because being acted on by, and so suffering with, *all* others.

I note in passing that this necessary dipolarity in the essential structure of God's very being corresponds to the essential duality or dipolarity of Christian faith in God, as comprising both the relatively more passive pole of unreserved trust or confidence in God and the relatively more active pole of unqualified loyalty or fidelity to God and to God's cause. It makes sense to summon human beings to unreserved trust or confidence in God if, and only if, God is unsurpassably active, doing all that anyone could conceivably do to optimize the conditions under which all must act and suffer the actions of others. Similarly, it is meaningful to call human beings to unqualified loyalty or fidelity to God—as the first and great commandment does—if, and only if, God is unsurpassably passive, suffering all that anyone could conceivably suffer to render the actions and sufferings of all everlastingly significant. Necessarily implied by this, I may point out, is not only my doctrine of faith, but also my doctrines of God as Creator and Consummator of all things, and therefore also Emancipator and Redeemer of the world, and hence also Savior of all human beings—indeed, of any beings who can understand and are therefore morally free—insofar as they accept the gift and demand of God's redemption. But I shall have more to say about these doctrines in subsequent discussions.

The conclusion of my argument in this section, then, is this: If Jesus is indeed who Christians assert him to be—namely, all-compassion, pure, unbounded love—then the strictly ultimate reality that radical monotheists call "God" can be rightly conceived only as the one strictly universal individual, whose being in itself, in its essential structure, is dipolar and who, therefore, can be rightly said to be the object of both the unreserved trust and the unqualified loyalty that are definitive of Christian faith.

This genuinely dipolar way of conceiving God, however, is not how God has usually been conceived in the Christian tradition. In the more *mythological* formulations in the tradition, God appears, sure enough, as a concrete individual, but only at the cost of not being strictly universal. On the other hand, in the more *metaphysical* formulations in the tradition, the utter universality of God does indeed find expression, but only by reducing God, in effect, to a sheer abstraction and obscuring God's unique individuality. In short, there are, as Hartshorne likes to say, "two forms of idolatry," not only one: not only the concrete idolatry of traditional mythology, but also the abstract idolatry of traditional metaphysics.[2]

I want to go back for a moment to the point about language. If God, as I have argued, is to be thought and spoken of literally as an *individual*, I have not said, nor should I wish to say, that God is to be thought and spoken of literally as a *person*. Why not? All talk of God as a person, I hold, is at best symbolic, not literal, talk. Its purpose, as of symbolic talk of God in general, is less intellectual or metaphysical than existential, less to describe the structure of God in itself than to express the meaning of God for us. Consequently, if such talk succeeds in its existential purpose of authorizing our existence in obedient faith, all well and good. If it doesn't, it can and should be dispensed with, in favor of other, more meaningful symbols. But if this is true of thinking and speaking of God as a person, it is true *a fortiori* of thinking and speaking of God as a *male* person, and also, naturally, as anything more specifically gender-specific such as "Father" or "King."

2.3. THE TRIUNE GOD: FATHER, SON, AND HOLY SPIRIT

In the preceding section, I have tried to clarify the sense in which a certain understanding of God is not only the most fundamental presupposition of Christian witness to Jesus as the Christ, but also its most important implication. But, for many persons both within and without the Christian tradition, to talk about the understanding of God necessarily implied by the Christian witness is to talk, above all, about the understanding of God as triune, three-in-one—in a word, as the trinity. Is it not necessary, then, to talk about the trinity if one is to talk Christianly about God?

The obvious answer is that it is, indeed, necessary, since so many of those who have preceded us in the Christian tradition have talked very much about the trinity and have even declared it to be necessary to do so for all who would be Christians. But my question is intended to press behind this obvious answer to inquire whether those who have gone before us are or are not justified in having done this. My response to the question is that it can be answered affirmatively only if, or insofar as, the specifically Christian experience out of which formally normative Christian witness arises also warrants or requires talking about God as triune.

2. See Hartshorne, "Two Forms of Idolatry."

A difficulty this response immediately raises, of course, is that what our experience warrants or requires us to talk about is always a function, in part, of the particular concepts and terms in which we alone can have our experience in the first place as an explicit conscious experience. Some philosophers have argued persuasively that we never encounter reality "except under a given description" (Nelson Goodman). But whether or not this is true without qualification, there is certainly no explicit understanding of anything without some *preunderstanding* of it; and it is rarely easy to determine what of our understanding of something derives from our actual experience of it and what derives, instead, from our preunderstanding—all the assumptions we bring with us, and have to bring with us, in order to understand it at all. For this reason, appeals to specifically Christian experience, even as to experience more generally, are never as conclusive as we may sometimes suppose them to be. It is always possible that what we in all good conscience make as an appeal to experience is little more than an appeal to the thought and speech of those who have gone before us, apart from our having already made use of which our experience would not be the experience we take it to be.

There is the further and, to my mind, far more telling consideration, however, that, if some of our Christian forebears have declared it necessary to talk about God as triune, by no means all of them have so spoken of God, much less declared such talk to be necessary. Not only is this obviously true of all of the New Testament writers—none of whom can be said to have a properly trinitarian conception of God without anachronism—but it is also, if perhaps less obviously, true of the early church fathers. According to the patristic scholar, Maurice Wiles, "The thought of the earliest [*sc.* Ante-Nicene] Fathers about God was not so unfailingly threefold in character that they were forced to think in trinitarian terms. Their thought about God was at least as much binitarian as trinitarian."[3]

But if one can hardly claim that we *must* speak of God as triune in order to spell out all the implications of the Christian witness for an understanding of God, perhaps one can claim that we *may* so speak of God—and maybe even have very good reasons for so speaking. Consider the following argument.

Every Christian so experiences God through Jesus as to be aware of God as the transcendental primal source authorizing her or his existence

3. Wiles, *Working Papers in Doctrine*, 9.

in obedient faith working through love and love incarnating itself as justice. But insofar, then, as authorizing in this case means both *entitling*, or giving the *right* to, existence in faith, and *empowering*, or giving the *power* so to exist, one may say that God is revealed at least implicitly to every Christian in her or his experience as such, as the triune God. In other words, Christians experience God as at once the primal source authorizing their existence in faith and love (God the Father); as the word conveying the right or entitlement to such existence (God the Son); and as the spirit bestowing the power or empowerment so to exist (God the Holy Spirit).

It will be noted, however, that I put all this conditionally, by saying that one would have reason thus to think and speak of God as triune *insofar as* God's authorization of our existence in faith may be properly analyzed as involving the two distinguishable moments of entitlement and empowerment respectively. My own judgment is that this condition is, in fact, satisfied. And yet, on any account, entitlement and empowerment are very closely related, and one might not unreasonably conclude that what is really yielded by thinking of God as the primal authorizing source of existence in faith and love is not so much a trinitarian as a binitarian understanding. I am not myself greatly troubled by this conclusion, because I have no interest whatever in arguing that we *have* to think of God as triune if we are to think of God Christianly. My point is only that we *may* so think of God; and I have tried to specify at least one way in which I would be willing to do so.

There is a closely related consideration that allows one to specify yet another such way. One may quite reasonably argue that, on a proper analysis of the primal source authorizing existence in faith, this source must have a *noetic* as well as an *ontic* aspect. The ontic aspect of the source is *God Godself*, in God's meaning for us, as decisively re-presented through Jesus. But its noetic aspect is *our own experience of God* as thus decisively re-presented. Unless and until we actually so experience God's love through Jesus as to know ourselves entitled and empowered by it to exist in faith, our existence in faith is not yet authorized—*for us*. The question, however, is how it is possible for us to have such an experience; and the answer to this question that faith itself requires, arguably, is that it is precisely God Godself who alone makes this possible. *Impossible est, sine Deo—discere Deo*—it is impossible to discern God without God. So God Godself must not only be on the ontic side of the primal source of

34

authorization, as the *object* of our experiencing, but must also be on its noetic side, as the *subject* but for whose empowering presence we ourselves neither would nor could be subjects of this experience as well. Of course, the same kind of question can be raised here as we allowed in distinguishing between the moments of entitlement and empowerment in the concept of authority. To what extent is the distinction between the ontic and the noetic sides of the primal authorizing source of Christian existence sufficiently clear and sharp to warrant distinguishing God the Son as well as God the Father on its ontic side and God the Holy Spirit on its noetic side as the divine empowerment but for which it neither would nor could have a noetic side for us?

Even so, it is in some such ways as this that I would be willing to reformulate the so-called economic trinity, or "trinity of revelation," by which is meant the trinity yielded by reflection on the basic experience of each and every Christian in coming to faith. I would want to allow, however, that neither of the distinctions on which I have relied—between entitlement and empowerment and between the ontic and noetic sides of the primal authorizing source—may be sufficiently clear and sharp to yield a real, more than merely verbal or conceptual, distinction between God the Son and God the Holy Spirit.

There remains the question, in any case, of the so-called immanent, or essential, trinity, or, as it is also called sometimes, "the ontological trinity." By this is meant the trinity that Christian theologians have traditionally held God to be in Godself, in God's own essential being, as distinct from God in God's revelation of Godself to us. May one also think and speak of God as triune in *this* sense?

I believe one may, although here, too, I would resist any claim that one must. All that one is required to say Christianly about God's own essential being is what follows necessarily from God's revelation of Godself to us decisively through Jesus. But, if I am right, the legitimate motive in even the most speculative doctrines of the immanent trinity lies precisely here. We believe as Christians that the God in whom we believe is nothing other or less than God Godself. Therefore, if God is revealed to us as triune, and if this revelation is, as we believe, the revelation of God's own essential being, and not a mere appearance of God, or something merely accidental in God, then God is and must be triune in Godself as well as in God's self-revelation. *Mutatis mutandis*, one may say that if we *may* think and speak of God as triune for us on the basis of our Christian experience of God decisively through Jesus, then we *may* also think and speak of God as triune in Godself.

But just how is God to be thought and spoken of as triune in this sense on the basis of an understanding of God as the primal source authorizing, i.e., entitling and empowering, our own existence in faith working through love? If God is, as I contend, the one strictly universal individual, whose essence, in symbolic terms, is "all compassion, pure, unbounded love," then God may be said to be at once the universal subject and the universal object of love. God loves all things, Godself as well as all others, and all things are, insofar as they are at all, only because or insofar as each of them, in its way, loves God, or is somehow internally related to God, and so participates in God's love. But, then, the essential being of God has a definite threefold structure, in that God is (1) the primordial *unity* of loving and being loved by all things, Godself as well as all others (God the Father); and their primordial *difference*, i.e., both (2) the one integral *object* of all love, of God's own love as well as of the love of all others (God the Son), and (3) the one all-inclusive *subject* of love, of Godself as well as of everything else (God the Holy Spirit). It is in some such way as this that God, in my view, may be said to be triune not only in God's revelation to us, but also in God's own essential being.

Incidentally, I could put this in the terms of more traditional doctrines of the trinity as follows: In the one act of loving all things, Godself as well as all others, God the Father both "generates" God the Son as the integral object of God's love, *in and with* whom God loves all other things; and, through God the Son, actively "spirates" God the Holy Spirit as the all-inclusive subject of God's love, *by* whom God loves all things.

But now, in my view, this same act of love whereby internally (*ad intra*) God is triune in Godself as well as in God's self-revelation is externally (*ad extra*) God's creation and consummation of some world of creatures other than and distinct from Godself. So, since in the nature of the case, nothing can be consummated that is not first created, the next topic to be considered, logically, once the doctrine of God has been developed to the point to which we have now come, is creation.

3

On Creation

3.1. THE MEANING OF "CREATION"

A S IT IS ORDINARILY used in Christian witness and theology, "creation" may mean either or both of two different, though closely related, things.

It may mean, first of all, the act or activity of God *ad extra* without which nothing other than God can come to be. And it may mean, secondly, the sum-total of things other than God, otherwise called "the world," understood as inclusive of both the self and all others, actual and possible. Relative to the first meaning of the term, "creation" is the act or activity of God because of which God is properly called "*the* Creator," in the sense of the sole *primal* source of all things. Relative to the second meaning of the term, "creation" includes all the creatures, possible as well as actual, that God, as their sole primal source, or as the Creator, either has created, is creating, or will create. Thus, from the standpoint of Christian witness and theology, to be anything at all is either to be God or to be a creature of God: either the Creator through whose eminent creativity everything else either was, is, or can be or else to be a creature of this Creator, a product of creation in the first sense of the term and a part of creation in the second sense

In developing the Christian understanding of God, I was careful to begin with the Christian witness and specifically with the christological assertion constituting it, i.e., the assertion that Jesus is of decisive significance for human existence because he is the decisive re-presentation of the meaning of God for us, and hence of the meaning of strictly ultimate reality for us. Presupposing, then, the claim of radical monotheism that *God* is strictly ultimate reality, and, conversely, that strictly ultimate reality is God, I tried to spell out what this christological assertion necessarily

37

implies for our understanding of God, given the further assumption that Jesus himself means love. This same basic procedure of spelling out the necessary implications of the Christian witness and of its christological assertion of Jesus' decisive significance must now be followed in all that is to be said on all other theological topics, including the present topic of creation. What follows, then, for an understanding of creation in both senses of the word if Jesus is the decisive re-presentation of the meaning of God for us?

3.2. CREATION AND EMANCIPATION

It may be recalled from what I said about the Christian doctrine of God that, in order to be the object of both the unreserved trust and the un-qualified loyalty that are definitive of Christian faith, God must be the one universal individual who is the sole primal source and the sole final end of all things. In other words, God must be the Creator and the Consummator, and so the Emancipator and the Redeemer, of everything else that exists. God must not only give an abiding meaning to everything that in itself is fleeting, and in this sense redeem it from what Paul calls its "bondage to decay" (Rom 8:21), but God must also make all things factually possible in the first place, as parts of an ordered world. By this I mean a world of creatures in which, by virtue of God's creative-emancipative ordering, the ratio of opportunity to risk for the creative activity of the creatures themselves is a favorable ratio—there being more possibilities for good to result from the creatures' own creativity than possibilities of evil.

But if something like this would perhaps be accepted by many, if not most, Christian theologians today, even as in the past, they would probably further agree that God's activity *ad extra*, as the Creator and the Consummator, and so the Emancipator and the Redeemer, of all things, is completely free and gratuitous. In creating, for example, God effects the transition from the wholly abstract, indeterminate possibility of *some* world or other to the more concrete, determinate possibility—the *factual* possibility—of *this* world or that. The clear implication of this logically, however, is that there must then be contingency both in God Godself and in the world, since, if God's creative act is indeed free and gratuitous, then it could have been otherwise than it in fact is, and the same could be true of the world that God creates by it. But already here there are serious difficulties in classical Christian theology, insofar as, denying what I have called the essential dipolarity of God, classical theologians have typically denied that there either is or could be anything contingent in God at all. And so we have the well-known paradoxes of a wholly necessary God being the utterly free and gratuitous Creator of a wholly contingent world.

But, more than that, classical theologians, and many who still follow them, have commonly assumed that, if God has the *positive* freedom to create this possible world or that, God must also have the wholly *negative* freedom not to create any world at all. The difficulties with this assumption, however, are equally, if not more, serious. For what is the point of God's having the freedom not to do something that it is better for God to do than not to do? Since any world is better than no world at all (there being no value whatever in nonentity), it would be either wrong or foolish of God not to create *some* world if God had the power to create it. But it contradicts the whole logic of the idea of God as unsurpassable to suppose that God could ever act either wrongly or foolishly. Of course, on some classical views of God, all possible value is already actualized in God's own being, anyhow, no matter what else may or may not exist, or whether anything else exists at all. But if this means that it is not better for God to have creatures than not to have them, since in either case God already possesses all possible value, then it also means that creatures really have no ultimate value at all, since by existing they add nothing whatever to God's eternal value. In this case, our own lives as creatures are ultimately as pointless as every other created thing. But, surely, this is counterintuitive if anything is and therefore nothing that any of us could coherently believe to be true, since our very act of believing it would imply its falsity, insofar as believing what is true instead of what is false would not itself be pointless but have a point.

There are good reasons, therefore, why at least some theologians have concluded that, just as there must be contingency both in God and in the world with respect to creation, so must there also be necessity with respect both to God's act as the Creator and to the world resulting from God's action, i.e., to creation in the second sense of the word. In other words, although both God's act of creating and any world that God creates are indeed completely free and gratuitous, and therefore wholly contingent rather than in any way necessary, nevertheless God, being all wise and all good as well as all-powerful, not only does but must create *some* world of creatures, and therefore some world of creatures could not conceivably fail to exist.

To be sure, the only reason for this "*must*" is God's own essential being as God—as all compassion, pure, unbounded love, and so the universal individual who is at once unsurpassably active and unsurpassably passive, or receptive of the actions of all others, and therefore unsurpassably wise and good as well as powerful. As such, God is in need of nothing that God's own essential nature as God could conceivably fail to provide; and God needs nothing for any reason other than God's own essential nature as the all-encompassing love that is all-wise and all-good and all-powerful. Those who take this position fully recognize, to be sure, that you and I might never have existed, that the earth that is our home might never have existed, that our solar system and galaxy might never have existed, even, indeed, that the present cosmic epoch of the universe might never have existed. For God alone exists necessarily, without any conceivable alternative. But these theologians deny that it in any way follows from this that God might ever have been all alone, because there might not have been anything other than God. They argue, on the contrary, that, if God is indeed all compassion, pure, unbounded love, it is more reasonable to believe that God's unsurpassable creative power is bound always to create some world or other, even though any world that God ever creates is and must be a wholly contingent rather than in any way a necessary world, just as God's act in creating it, being utterly free and gratuitous, is likewise contingent. God Godself is bound to exist, but not I myself or you yourself, or our world itself, or anything else itself. All that is bound to exist other than God is *some* world of creatures, none of which, however, either exists or could exist necessarily, but only contingently.

One contemporary Christian theologian who takes something more or less like this kind of a position is John Macquarrie, in his *Principles of Christian Theology*.[1] But, then, I myself am another, because any other position seems to me inconsistent with the Christian witness and its constitutive christological assertion, on whose necessary implications Christian theology has the task of critically reflecting. Given that assertion, creation in both senses of the word must be in one respect necessary, even as it is in another respect contingent, provided that the "all compassion, pure, unbounded love" of others, whose gift and demand are decisively re-presented to us through Jesus is no mere appearance, or nothing

---

1. Macquarrie, *Principles of Christian Theology*, 211–38.

merely accidental in God, but is God's very essence and therefore strictly necessary.

Of course, God's love for any particular others could only be contingent, holding, as I do, that God alone exists necessarily, all other individuals and events existing or occurring merely contingently. In this respect, God's love for others and the creation and consummation that are its two essential aspects must themselves also be contingent. But if God is not merely accidentally love of others and essentially love only of self—and this, I maintain, is what the christological assertion necessarily implies if Jesus' material meaning for us is love—then that there are always *some* others for God to love and that God, accordingly, is always the Creator of these others as well as their Consummator, are precisely not contingent but necessary. In this respect, the existence of the world, of *some* world, unlike the existence of the self, is strictly ultimate; and the concept "the world," understood as referring to the necessarily nonempty class of all realities other than God, any of whose members exists or occurs merely contingently, is strictly correlative with the concept "God."

The standard way of accepting the premise of this argument—that God is by God's very essence love of others—even while rejecting its conclusion—that some world of others must be as necessary as God is—is to argue that God, being triune, is indeed essentially love of others, but that the only necessary "others" are God Godself as three-in-one. But I see little, if anything, to recommend any such attempt to salvage the classical doctrine that God could exist and, in fact, once did exist all alone, without any world of creatures at all. For either God's love of Godself as triune preserves the essential truth of the fundamental presupposition of radical monotheism, in which case God is one and God's love of Godself is merely self-love rather than also love of others; or else God's love of Godself as triune really is love of others and not merely of self, in which case the essential truth of radical monotheism is lost by affirming a monotheism that is only verbally distinguishable from tritheism. Moreover, the problem remains that either some world is better than none, in which case God could fail to create some world only by being wrong or foolish or surpassable in creative power, or else our own existence and all existence is ultimately pointless, as none of us either believes or ever could believe if the measure of our belief is not what we say but what we do.

Because, however, creation in both senses of the word is necessary in one respect as well as contingent in another, the traditional doctrine of "creation out of nothing by God" (*creatio ex nihilo a Deo*) cannot be understood to imply an absolute beginning either of God's creative activity as such or of some world of creatures as such, both of which are strictly ultimate and therefore without beginning. Instead, "creation out of nothing by God" must be understood to mean that there is a beginning to *each and every particular world or creature*, even as of God's particular act of creating it and that, therefore, there once was when any creature or world was not because God had not as yet created it. Therefore, every particular world or creature that is so much as possible participates not only in the eminent being of God (*a Deo*) but also in the absolute nothing of not existing at all (*ex nihilo*). Even if it at some point comes to be, there once was when it was not and, from every indication, there eventually will be when it won't be any more.

Inasmuch, however, as any creature or world can come into being only by participating in the eminent being of God, it is and must be more or less like God. To be absolutely unlike God would be to be absolutely unlike being itself, and to be absolutely unlike being itself would be, self-contradictorily, to be nothing, everything that is anything at all being more than mere nothing thanks only to its participation in God and therefore being insofar forth like God Godself. Thus there is a definite sense in which not only woman and man, but also any creature, and any kind of creature whatever, is created in God's image, although, as we shall see, there is also a distinctive sense in which human beings alone can be said to be created *imago Dei*.

But this means that anything that is, is also *good*, because in participating in the being of God, it also participates in God's goodness, God's being and goodness being, as the scholastics said, "convertible," or, as we may prefer to translate, "coextensive." All things are essentially good by reason of *their* participation in God. On the other hand, all things are also essentially *holy* by reason of God's all-loving participation in them—just this participation by God in the being of the entire creation being what is properly meant by its "consummation" in God and its "redemption by God," i.e., the other essential aspect of the same divine love that is also essentially "creation" and "emancipation," or, as would be said in traditional terms, "creation" and "providence."

Having introduced this traditional distinction, however, I hasten to say that it ceases to be a clear and sharp, or, at any rate, necessary, distinction once one rejects the notion of an absolute beginning of creation in both senses of the word: both as God's creative activity and as the world of creatures created by God. Because the world as such has no absolute beginning, although each and every creature in the world begins, as does the divine creative act whereby any creature comes to be, creation cannot be adequately distinguished from providence in the traditional threefold sense of (1) God's *preservation* of all creatures once created; (2) God's *concurrence* with these creatures in their own creative actions; and (3) God's *governance* of the whole process of creaturely creativity. This is not to deny, however, that much that has been said in traditional discussions of providence can and should find its place in an adequately developed doctrine of creation.

Moreover, there is at least this distinction that definitely can be made in the case of any creaturely individual or aggregate of individuals enduring through time. In any such case, there is a difference between any individual or aggregate's coming into existence as such, as just this individual or aggregate, and its coming to exist in just this, that, or some other particular state at any point "in between" its beginning to be at all and its ceasing to be altogether. Thus, for example, there is a difference between the coming into existence of the particular human individual that I am and to which my proper name correctly refers and this same individual's coming to exist in a particular state or condition, such as the one in which I presently find myself, seated at my desk in my study writing these sentences, instead of being about any of the many other things I am also accustomed to doing. Or, again, there is a somewhat similar difference between the coming into existence of the vast aggregate of individuals and events that we refer to as "our solar system" and that same aggregate's coming to exist in some particular state or condition, such as it was in, say, after the emergence on earth of a number of species of primate vertebrates, but before the emergence of any specifically hominoid forms of life. Corresponding to this difference, then, one can clearly distinguish, if one wishes, between creation and providence as acts of God necessary respectively either to the sheer coming into existence of an individual or an aggregate, in the case of creation, or to its coming to exist in each and every state or condition in which it comes to exist, in the case of providence.

I may add, incidentally, that a corresponding and equally clear distinction may be made between consummation and redemption as acts of God having to do respectively with God's being the sole final *end* of

43

all things as well as their sole primal source. Whereas the term "consummation" refers properly to God's activity with respect to each and every individual or aggregate consequent upon its ceasing to exist as such or at all, "redemption" refers properly to God's activity with respect to each individual or aggregate consequent upon its ceasing to exist in just this, that, or some other actual state or condition.

So far as the further traditional distinction between general and special providence is concerned, I have no real use for it because I think of all providence as special, in that God continually acts anew in response to the actions of each and every creature in such a way as ever and again to re-establish the optimal conditions for the creature's own action in solidarity with all of its fellow creatures. But some are sure to ask, If this is all there is to special providence, what about "extraordinary providence," or so-called miracles, in the sense of special divine interventions over and above the kind of providential action I have just described? So far as I am concerned, the problem with miracles in this sense is not whether God can or would ever perform them. Believing, as I do, that God is strictly unsurpassable in wisdom, goodness, and power, I unhesitatingly infer that, if things in the cosmos would be better managed by God's so intervening, God could and would most certainly intervene. But I dispute the competence of any human being to judge whether or not this condition is ever satisfied, and I believe that the reports of such interventions in the Christian tradition are more reasonably accounted for in other ways—especially by taking them to be what the author of the Fourth Gospel suggestively calls "signs."

I do hold, however (and have explained at length elsewhere), that one may very well speak of God's creative activity as *emancipative* as well as creative, and in *that* sense as "liberation," the other sense of "liberation" properly expressing God's activity as "*redemptive*."[2] Because the creative activity of God is but the other essential aspect of the same unsurpassable love of all others that is also consummative, God's creative power over others is omnibeneficent, or all-good, even as it is omnipotent, or all-powerful. Consequently, God's only aim or intention in exercising God's power is to secure the best possible self-creation of all creatures as one and all contributors to God's own self-creation as God, and, in this sense, to God's glory. Thus God unfailingly exercises God's power to optimize the

2. See Ogden, *Faith and Freedom*, 68–79.

limits of the creatures' own free decisions, by setting such limits to their self-creation and creation of others that, if the limits were to be different, the ratio of opportunity for good to risk of evil would not be as favorable. This God does by establishing such fundamental limits of cosmic order, or, as we commonly say, "natural laws," that, if the creatures were allowed either more or less freedom than these limits allow, there would be more chances of evil than of good resulting from their actions, instead of the other way around. For this reason, however, God's creative activity is by its very nature emancipative, in that, establishing the optimal limits of all creatures' freedom, it thereby sets them free to create themselves and one another.

Among the other things this implies, I should note, is that God's creative or emancipative activity very definitely "takes sides," insofar as God always acts so as to maximize the opportunities for good, while minimizing the risks of evil. Consequently, even though God's love of others, and hence God's acceptance of them, is boundless, God's *acceptance* of everything in no way implies God's *approval* of everything, and God's approval of anything is, in truth, strictly bounded by the unsurpassable goodness of God's aim: that each creature individually and all creatures together should enjoy the best possible self-creations as imperishable contributions to God's own divine glory.

3.3. THE QUESTION OF EVIL

But what about the reality of evil? Important for any theological treatment of this question is the distinction that has sometimes been made between "metaphysical evil" and "factual evil" and the further distinction, as regards the two main types of the second, between "natural evil" (*malum physicum*) and "moral evil" (*malum morale*). By "metaphysical evil" is meant the evil, or, as I would argue, the so-called evil, that belongs to all creaturely existence as such—the price that must be paid, if you will, if there is to be any creaturely, and hence contingent, existence at all. By "natural evil" and "moral evil," on the other hand, are meant respectively the two types of the evil that results from factual choices, whether creaturely or divine, or somehow both, above and beyond the sheer metaphysical reality of creaturely existence.

Moral evil is different from natural evil in that it results from factual choices involving distinctively moral freedom, i.e., the special, high-level kind of freedom that human beings alone, among earth's creatures, are presently known to possess. It follows from the unsurpassable goodness of God that both types of factual evil are due entirely to creaturely choices, in no way to divine choices, so far as the *actuality* of such evil is concerned, although the *factual possibility* of evil, like the factual possibility of good, is due to divine choices, also, and indeed primarily so.

Factual evil involves the relative loss of concrete good, which can happen for one or the other of two opposing reasons: either because conflict between goods is avoided only at the price of boredom or monotony; or because monotony of goods is avoided only at the price of conflict. Thus what is meant by good in contrast with evil is the realization of concrete unity-in-variety, or the concrete harmony of goods—*the community of good*, if you will—that is actuality itself.

I may note in this connection that, among the other difficulties I have with so-called anthropocentric approaches to the doctrine of creation, not the least serious is the claim that all natural evil is somehow the result of human sin or moral evil. As someone who has increasingly suffered to some extent from arthritis, I have taken more than casual notice of the findings of some vertebrate paleontologists that the fossils of the joints of certain dinosaurs clearly evidence their having been more or less seriously arthritic. So far as I am concerned, the arthritis from which a dinosaur suffered long before it could have conceivably been due somehow to human sin was and remains an evil without which the present cosmic epoch of the universe would have been a better place than it in fact was and is, not only for the dinosaur and all other creatures in any way affected by it, but also, and above all, for God. Of course, my Christian faith in God leads me to believe that God would not have allowed even the factual possibility of the dinosaur's arthritis unless precluding it would have made for a less than optimal ordering of the ratio between opportunities for good and risks of evil as a result of the creatures' own actions. I also believe, with, among others, Thomas Aquinas, that the only irredeemable evil, from a Christian standpoint, is the loss of the possibility of the creature's being redeemed by and consummated in God, who is not only the Creator and the Emancipator, and hence the sole primal source of all things, but also the Consummator and the Redeemer, and hence the sole final end of all things. In the case of human creatures, who, as I have said—and will presently be explaining—are uniquely created in God's image, God's redemption and consummation are and must be mediated through their own distinctive kind of freedom and responsibility, which is to say, their *moral* freedom and responsibility. This means that their lives can be redeemed and consummated in the proper sense of the words if, and only if, they are also *saved*, i.e., only if they themselves so accept God's free acceptance of them through obedient faith, and thus through trusting in God's love and being loyal to it alone, that they exist in authentic freedom both from themselves and the world and for themselves and God's cause. Relative, then, to *this* final human end of being saved or lost, all other evils, however real and serious, are not irredeemable but redeemable. Put differently—and in terms perhaps approximating the human-centered approaches I am criticizing—all other evils are themselves irredeemable only if or insofar as they are the occasions for the one irredeemable evil of allowing oneself to be separated from God, by persisting in refusing God's gracious acceptance through the obedience of faith. Nevertheless, this distinction between irredeemable and redeemable evil is not at all the same as the distinction between *real* evil, on the one hand, and merely *apparent* evil, on the other, as anthropocentric approaches to the doctrine of creation typically seem to represent it as being.

So far as the so-called *problem* of evil is concerned, my position is that it is really a pseudo-problem in that it only arises given certain of the untenable assumptions of classical theism, which are incoherent in themselves quite apart from the fact of evil. Specifically, the implication that "omnipotent," or "all-powerful," means all the power there is, is self-incoherent in that "power" is by definition a *social* concept through and through. By this I mean that any coherently conceivable power, however great, necessarily presupposes at least *some* other power in relation to which it is exercised. Accordingly, if "omnipotence" is a coherent concept at all, it cannot mean all the power there is, but only all the power that any one individual could conceivably have, given the existence of other individuals having the power over which omnipotent power can alone be exercised. So to understand omnipotence, however, is already to have escaped from the alleged trilemma of either (1) denying that God is all-powerful; (2) denying that God is all-good; or (3) denying that evil is real. Although God is unsurpassable in both power and goodness, and thus is all-powerful as well as all-good in the only coherent senses of the words, evil can be and is real because of the real power of creatures, also, to make decisions—decisions that God does not make and cannot make, not because God's power is somehow limited, or "finite," but solely and simply because to be at all and to have some power, however minimal, are simply two ways of talking about one and the same thing.

3.4. HUMAN EXISTENCE

3.4.0. Preliminary Remarks

Here, too, even as in the doctrines of God and creation in general, the procedure we have to follow is to begin with normative Christian witness, and specifically with its constitutive christological assertion, and then inquire as to the necessary implications, as well as the presuppositions, of this assertion. If Jesus is the decisive re-presentation of the meaning of ultimate reality for us, and if Jesus means love, what does this necessarily presuppose and imply about human existence?

I shall attempt to answer this question by considering three main topics: (1) the chief defining characteristics of human existence; (2) the senses of "sin"; and (3) the human predicament. This assumes that the "human existence" that is the general topic of this section covers both what we *essentially* are and cannot fail to be as soon and as long as we are human beings at all *and* what we are *existentially*, in the state or condition in which we actually find ourselves insofar as we exist as human beings have apparently existed in fact, everywhere and always, throughout human history.

3.4.1. The Chief Defining Characteristics of Human Existence

Normative Christian witness presupposes or implies four main claims about the defining characteristics of human existence.

The first is that to be human, just as to be anything else other than God, is to be God's creature and hence to be created out of nothing by God. Thus, radically unlike God, who alone exists necessarily, woman and man exist contingently, in that there once was when they were not, and their existence as creatures is always marked by their participation not only in the relative nothing of unrealized possibility, but also in the absolute nothing of not existing at all. Nonetheless, woman and man also participate, in their way, in the being of God and are therefore also essentially good in that, like all other creatures in the world, they thereby share in God's own uncreated goodness. So the great Renaissance thinker and churchman, Nicholas of Cusa, goes so far as to refer to the world, as "created God" (*Deus creatus*) and to a human being as "occasioned God" and "humaned God" (*Deus occasionatus* and *Deus hominatus*).[3]

The second claim of the Christian witness is that woman and man participate in the being and goodness of God in a distinctive way—namely, not only by being somehow related to them internally, as any creature is, or even by being related to them experientially, so as to experience or feel them, as all animals, at least, presumably do, but also by being related to them *understandingly*, and therefore with distinctively moral freedom and responsibility. Thus, to be human is not only to be analogous to God in the way in which anything whatever has to be if it is to exist at all, but also to be, in a unique sense, the "image of God" (*imago Dei*).

In orthodox theology, one of the implications of being thus uniquely created in God's image is that human beings are given the "dominion over the earth" (*dominium terræ*) spoken of in Genesis 1:26ff., where God is made to say: "Let us make human beings in our image, after our likeness, and let them have dominion over the fish of the sea, and over the birds of the air, and over the cattle, and over all the earth, and over every creeping thing that creeps upon the earth." As a general rule, theologians have traditionally understood this dominion to refer to the right and power of human beings to rule—not only over all the other creatures on earth, but also over themselves individually and, in the case, at least, of a select few of the wise and the holy, also over their fellow human beings. But faced as we now are with the down- as well as the up-side of the growing human domination of the rest of nature, not to mention one another, we are likely to want to know just wherein this right and power of human beings to rule consists.

It consists, I suggest, in their having the authority, and so both the right and the power, to establish, maintain, and transform "the smaller, *local* orders that we properly speak of as 'societies' and 'cultures,'" even as God's own unique and archetypal rule, of which theirs is but the image, consists in establishing, maintaining, and transforming "the larger, *cosmic* order of nature."[4] Of course, the order established by human societies and cultures pertains most immediately and directly to human beings. But, as we are now all too acutely aware, it also impacts all the other creatures on earth—and, as now appears, wherever else human beings extend their

3. Dolan, ed., *Unity and Reform*, 41–42.

4. Ogden, *Faith and Freedom*, 77.

dominion. The merit of this suggestion, I think, is that it understands our human dominion in terms of the specifically *political* aspect of our moral freedom and responsibility as human beings, not only to act within social and cultural structures but also to create these structures themselves.

The third claim about the defining characteristics of human beings that the Christian witness implies is that, being in this unique sense created in God's *image* (*imago*), we are thereby given and called to exist also in God's *likeness* (*similitudo*)—the first sometimes also being said to constitute the *formal* image of God in us, the second, God's *material* image. Thus, to be human means that, as creatures of God, we either are or can be uniquely the image of God in a double sense. Insofar as we are human at all, we are understanding and, therefore, morally free and responsible beings. Accordingly, even after the fall, or in the state or condition of sin, each of us is and remains created in God's image in the first, formal or, as it is also called, *general*, sense (*imago Dei generaliter*). But we are all also given and called to be the image of God in the second, material or *special* sense (*imago Dei specialiter*), in that we are given and called to live in the authentic freedom of obedient faith working through love. It is in this same sense, however, that we can also lose the image of God; and, according to the Christian witness, it is our actual state or condition as human beings always already thus to have lost our authentic being through sin and to stand in need of its restoration by God's grace to us decisively through Jesus Christ.

A fourth claim that normative Christian witness implies about our being human is that our being thus created in God's image includes the categorial level of our *life-praxis*, of leading our lives by what we ourselves think, say, and do, and also the transcendental level of our *self-understanding*, of how we each understand ourselves in both the immediate and the ultimate settings of our lives. How we understand ourselves in our ultimate setting, especially in relation to strictly ultimate reality, has implications both for all that we are to believe about ourselves and everything else and for all that we are to do in relation to the interests affected by our actions, of all others as well as ourselves. The reason for this is that we are not simply selves, but *embodied* selves related to others, who exist only in a world together with other beings and kinds of beings, both human and other than human. Thus, although as selves we transcend, in an important way, both our bodies and our social relations to other selves, we are never ourselves apart from them; and how we understand ourselves has implications for what we believe and how we act, including all that we do in relation to others.

I would underscore that the distinction just made between understanding ourselves at the transcendental level and leading our lives at the categorial level (i.e., between self-understanding and life-praxis) is fundamental to clarifying any number of concepts and distinctions that have proved to be more or less indispensable to doing Christian theology. Thus, for example, the traditional theological concept "faith" is to be clarified, purely formally, as "authentic self-understanding," just as "good works," or "witness," are, purely formally, matters of "life-praxis." Or, again, "sin" (in the singular and in the proper theological sense) is, formally, "inauthentic self-understanding," while "sins" (in the plural), as we are about to learn, properly refers, in one use of "sin," to the expressions of inauthentic self-understanding in "life-praxis."

3.4.2. The Senses of "Sin"

The term "sin" (in the singular), used absolutely and without qualification, can be defined both negatively and positively. Negatively defined, it is "the privation or lack of original righteousness" (*privatio s. carentia iustitiæ originalis*); positively defined, it is the corruption or perversion of one's humanness that consists in being—in Martin Luther's phrase—"turned in upon oneself" (*incurvatus in se*). At its root, sin is negatively *unfaith*, which is to say, distrust in and disloyalty to God alone as the primal source and the final end of one's own being and of all beings, while positively sin is *idolatry*, that is, trust in and loyalty to someone or something alongside God as essential to one's own being and meaning, if not to the being and meaning of all other things as well. Thus the lack of original righteousness that consists in the perversion or corruption of one's human nature grows out of unfaith and idolatry. Orthodox theologians have commonly identified what grows out of unfaith and idolatry more exactly as "pride" (*superbia*), "self-love" (*amor sui*), and "desire" (*concupiscentia*).

By the term "original sin" (*peccatum originale*), then, is meant sin as a state or condition of human existence, i.e., the inauthentic *mode* of existence that consists in the self-*mis*understanding of God's love as the sole primal source and the sole final end of one's life even as of everything else. As such, original sin is one of the two original human possibilities "before God" (*coram Deo*), the other such possibility being "original righteousness" (*iustitia originalis*), which is the authentic mode of existence that consists in understanding oneself and the world in terms of God's love as their sole primal source and sole final end.

The term "actual sin" in the singular (*peccatum actuale*) is to be understood as the act whereby the possibility of inauthentic existence is and must be actualized by one's own self-misunderstanding before God. Thus there is a paradoxical, or dialectical, relationship between original sin as the state, condition, or *mode* of inauthentic existence and actual sin as the *act* necessary to one's existing in such a, state, condition, or mode. Exactly the same kind of relationship, by the way, exists between faith as the other state, condition, or mode, of authentic existence and the love through which faith works or is enacted—as well as between what Paul sometimes speaks of as "living by the Spirit" and "walking by the Spirit" (Gal 5:25). *Living* by the Spirit is the state, condition, or mode of existing authentically. But one cannot exist in that state, condition, or mode except by actually *walking* by the Spirit, and so existing authentically.

By "actual sins" in the plural (*peccata actualia*), finally, is properly meant sin as the plurality of acts—of thoughts, words, and deeds—that both express one's own sinful self-misunderstanding and misrepresent it to others as their authentic possibility, too.

To this all-too brief clarification of the different senses of "sin," I may add just a note on the relation of sin to what I spoke of in sec. 3.3 above as "moral evil." The relation is a bit complicated because the term "moral" and its cognates are also properly used in more than one sense. In a broad sense, anything may be distinguished as "moral" that involves the distinctive level of creaturely freedom that I have called "moral freedom." Since sin, as I went on to argue, involves just such moral freedom, sin is rightly understood to be one form or level of moral evil—specifically, its *transcendental* form or level, where moral freedom is involved in the fundamental option between "faith" and "sin," or authentic and inauthentic self-understanding. Conventionally, however, sin (or sins) tend(s) to be identified simply with the other *categorial* form or level of moral evil, so that one is taken to be a sinner because, or insofar as, one transgresses the moral law, or does morally evil things, in this other, stricter sense of "morally evil." But this conventional view is profoundly misleading. Not only is sin in the singular, whether as original sin or as actual sin, not to be identified with moral evil in the categorial sense, but even sin in the plural, as actual sins, is not just another word for moral transgressions in this stricter sense of the term. If actual sins are defined as I have defined them, as expressions and representations of actual/original sin, they may very well include moral observances or moral good as well as moral transgressions or moral evil in the categorial sense. Think only of Thomas Becket's words in T. S. Eliot's *Murder in the Cathedral*, "The last temptation is the greatest treason:/ To do the right deed for the wrong reason." This is true, moreover, even if it is also true and very much worth emphasizing, that the sinner, just because or insofar as she or he *is* a sinner and therefore *acts* sinfully, is sure to commit moral evil in the categorial sense of moral transgressions—especially if the standard for judging such is not merely some conventional moral standard but God's radical demand of love and the commandments to do justice that it implies. This point, by the way, is one of the further implications of the fourth claim about the chief defining characteristics of human existence of which I spoke in sec. 3.4.1 above. This is the claim, it will be recalled, that distinguishes even as it relates the two levels of transcendental self-understanding, on the one hand, and categorial life-praxis, on the other.

3.4.3. *The Human Predicament*

The "profound corruption of human nature" brought about by sin is rightly understood as a universal fact, not as a modal necessity, although it is the latter understanding, unfortunately, that many traditional doctrines of sin have either asserted outright or in fact implied even if they have verbally denied it. According to the orthodox doctrine of "birth sin," because of which "the offspring of Adam" are *ipso facto* "not able not to sin" (*non posse non peccare*), the sin of all human beings, the original pair alone excepted, is a matter, self-contradictorily, not of freedom, but of fate or destiny—and, in this sense, of what I mean by "modal necessity."

I should perhaps explain that the modal schema I am presupposing in putting the matter this way is one that goes back to Augustine, who distinguishes all four of the states or conditions of human beings in modal terms, beginning with creation and ending in glory. In their first state, after their creation but before their fall, human beings are "able to sin" (*posse peccare*). In the second state, after their fall but before their redemption, they are "not able not to sin" (*non posse non peccare*). In the third state, after their redemption but before glory, they are "able not to sin" (*posse non peccare*). Finally, in the fourth state, the state of glory, they are "not able to sin" (*non posse peccare*).

Over against all such modal formulations, I take it to be essential to insist that the human predicament resulting from the fall be described purely factually, by the statistical generalization that: (1) every human being is continually inclined to misunderstand her- or himself before God; and (2) every human being is born into a humanity for which this generalization already holds good and which, therefore, in its thoughts, words, and deeds, and their complex institutionalization in societies and cultures, is already a profoundly corrupted humanity. Being a statistical generalization only, however, this way of putting the matter allows for the possibility of particular exceptions to the general rule. It still means, though, that, even if none of us can excuse her or his own sin by the sin and the sins of others, each of us must also answer to God for having caused her or his brothers and sisters to stumble, by tempting them to sin. Why? Well, because the possibility that we, as sinful women and men in this sense, continually re-present to one another is not the possibility of authentic faith, and thus of authentic love and hope, but instead the possibility of unfaith, and thus of lovelessness and despair. By our sin in the strict sense, we each *actualize* this possibility, whereas by our sin in the broad sense—the sense that includes our *sins* as well as our *sin*—we not only actualize it but also *misrepresent* it to others as *their* authentic possibility, also. In this sense, or to this extent, there is a deep truth in Augustine's depressing verdict that humankind is a "mass of perdition" (*massa perditionis*), and one may unhesitatingly agree with Paul Tillich that, in the case of every single one of us, "Sin is a universal fact before it becomes an individual act."[5]

Even apart from the fact of sin and its tragic universality, however, the human condition could still be aptly characterized as precisely a "predicament." This is true, first of all, because woman and man would still share fully in the universal predicament of all creatures simply as creatures, that, being radically contingent in existence as well as actuality, they could not but participate in the absolute nothing of not being at all and would remain ever exposed to its threat. But it is true, second, because, unlike other creatures, so far, at least, as we are acquainted with them, woman and man would have to endure this universal threat to all

5. Tillich, *Systematic Theology*, vol. 2, 56.

creaturely existence *understandingly*, with more or less conscious aware-ness of their own radical contingency and of the contingency of all other created things. All of us know if we know anything that the philosopher, Bertrand Russell, is exactly right, that "on us and all our race the slow, sure doom falls pitiless and dark." Because this is so, however, there is no need for the exaggerated anti-Pelagianism that would risk making sin neces-sary, or, as some would have it, "inevitable" (e.g., Reinhold Niebuhr), lest our human dependence on God and our profound need for God's love be supposed somehow not to be absolute but merely relative. As important as it certainly is for Christian witness and theology to maintain that our dependence on God and our need for God's love are and ever remain absolute, the appropriate way to do this is not by means of a seriously inadequate doctrine of sin, but rather by means of an adequate doctrine of creation such as the preceding discussion has sought to provide.

4

On Jesus Christ

4.0. PRELIMINARY REMARKS

BEFORE TURNING TO THE main topics of the doctrine of Jesus Christ, I want to make a few preliminary remarks on the procedure I have been trying to follow in the foregoing discussions of God and creation—as well as, indeed, of prolegomena.

That procedure, as I have described (and, I hope, followed) it, assumes the givenness of Christian witness and, specifically, of what I call its constitutive christological assertion. Beginning with this assertion, or, more exactly, with an interpretation of it that claims to agree with the formally normative witness of the apostles, I have sought to explicate both the possibility of self-understanding, or understanding of existence, of which it is the expression and the necessary presuppositions and implications of this possibility for what one is to believe and to do if one is to be a Christian. Thus, whether I have developed the doctrine of God or the doctrine of creation in general and of human existence in particular, this is the theological procedure I have been concerned to follow in doing so: to explicate, as best I can, "the truth as it is in Jesus."

But, as I have at several points remarked, I have had to proceed in doing all this far more dogmatically than I would have preferred, by simply assuming my interpretation of the christological assertion instead of arguing for it. I have assumed that this assertion functions *formally* to assert the decisive significance of Jesus for us, which is to say, for any and every human existent as such, and that what is meant *materially* by Jesus is, in Charles Wesley's words, "all compassion, pure, unbounded love," and therefore the explicit, indeed, decisive, authorization that we are to exist in obedient faith working through love and love incarnating itself in justice. Assuming this, then, I have tried to explicate the meaning of such an existence and to spell out its main presuppositions and implications for a Christian understanding of God and the world and of ourselves as God's good, if also fallen, creation.

The relevance of this to the present discussion is that the time has now come for me to argue for what I have hitherto simply assumed and asserted without reason—with respect both to the formal analysis of the christological assertion and to its material meaning, according to the formally normative witness of the apostles. This explains the first two of the three main sections of what follows, in which I shall begin by analyzing the christological assertion purely formally and then interpret its meaning materially, given the material identity of Jesus attested by the apostolic witness. In the third and final section, then, I shall make some concluding comments on the contemporary project of a christology of liberation and on how I, for one, should think to carry it out.

4.1. THE CONSTITUTIVE CHRISTOLOGICAL ASSERTION

I ask the reader to recall what I have already said about the christological assertion early in my discussion of the doctrine of God. Although there is only a slight overlap between those earlier statements and what I now propose to say, they should provide at least a helpful preunderstanding of my argument in this first section, which will proceed by three main steps.

4.1.1. *The Classical Formulation of the Assertion*

The first concerns what I call "the classical formulation of the christological assertion." In so speaking of it, I am implying that a distinction is always to be made between the christological assertion itself and any formulation of it, including its classical formulation. But although such a distinction can and should be made, it is nonetheless true that the christological assertion simply as such, all by itself, so to speak, is never a datum of theological reflection, but always only its object, or, if you will, its *objective*. By this I mean that the christological assertion is the one thing with which theology has to concern itself in critically appropriating all the many data that alone are ever actually given to it. In other words, the christological assertion is always given to theological reflection only in or as some particular formulation(s) that can never be simply identified with it, not even in the case of its normative or classical formulation. Thus, even in the formulation, "Jesus is the Christ," which probably has the best claim to be considered classical, theology has to distinguish between this formulation as such, which assumes the particular Jewish religious framework indicated by the term "the Christ," which is to say, "the Messiah," and the assertion that this formulation allows one to make, given these particular assumptions. But if this is true of *the* christological formulation *par excellence*—the one from which the term "christology" itself is derived—it is certainly true of all the other formulations through which, beginning with the apostles themselves, Christians have borne their distinctive witness by somehow asserting or implying one and the same constitutive christological assertion.

This can be put by saying that, although the christological assertion itself is *constant*, its formulations are *variable*. Always there is an assertion, and always it is an assertion about one and the same subject, which, as we shall see, asserts one and the same thing about this subject— namely, his decisive significance for human existence. But while any of the predicates asserted of the subject can serve to make this one constant assertion with its one constant point, the predicates themselves, and so the various formulations of the assertion, are many rather than one, and variable rather than constant. This can be brought out whenever writing "Jesus is the Christ" by setting "the Christ" in parentheses—so "Jesus is (the Christ)"—thereby indicating that it is but one, even if the classical, value of the predicate variable.

4.1.2. Principal Types of Christological Formulations

If we proceed now to take the next step, and ask about the principal types of christological formulations of which the history of Christian witness and theology provides examples, we must first distinguish between formulations that are only *implicitly* christological, because they do not actually make the christological assertion but merely imply it, and yet other formulations that are *explicitly* christological, because, in some way or other, and in some concepts-terms or other, they assert explicitly that Jesus is of decisive significance for human existence.

Among the examples of implicit christology to be found in the earliest Christian witness that, in my judgment, is to be taken as properly apostolic, and therefore formally normative, the following are representative:

The blind receive their sight, the lame walk, the lepers are cleansed, the deaf hear, the dead are raised, and the poor have good news brought to them. And blessed is anyone who takes no offense at me. (Matt 11:4ff.)

See, something greater than Solomon is here! . . . See, something greater than Jonah is here. (Luke 11:31ff.)

Whoever acknowledges me before others, the Son of Man also will acknowledge before the angels of God; but whoever denies me before others will be denied before the angels of God. (Luke 12:8–9)

An early example of explicit christology, by contrast, is the assertion implied by Peter's confession at Cæsarea Philippi, according to Matthew 16:15–16: "You are the Christ [i.e., the Messiah], the Son of the living God."

It has long since become clear from studies in historical theology, especially of the New Testament, that there is growing agreement among scholars that the first christology—whether it be taken to be the christology of the earliest witnesses or the christology of Jesus himself—was a merely implicit, rather than an explicit christology. One is led to this conclusion by the fact that there is no explicit christology evident in the earliest stratum of Christian witness and that, even in the synoptic gospels themselves, in the final form in which we now have them, there is relatively little explicit christology, as compared, say, with the Fourth Gospel, or even with the much earlier letters of Paul and of others in the Pauline tradition to whom we presumably owe Colossians and Ephesians as well as 2 Thessalonians. Of course, if this widely shared conclusion is correct, we find ourselves in the curious situation of having to work with a formally normative Christian witness, in the earliest witness now accessible to us, that is not explicitly but only implicitly christological. This means that what all subsequent Christian witness with its more or less explicit christology has to be in substantial agreement with in order to have a valid claim to be appropriate does not itself contain any explicit christology at all, however much its formulations may definitely imply such.

But beyond this first basic distinction between implicit and explicit christology, we also need to distinguish between different main types of explicit christology itself. One such distinction that is often made, particularly in work informed by the history of religions contemporary with, and in the environment of, early Christianity, is the distinction between christological formulations whose principal assumptions are traditionally Jewish and still other formulations that assume one or the other of the many religious outlooks of non-Jewish origin that were also present in the pluralistic cultural world of the late Hellenistic ecumene. In fact, this distinction has been shown to be important even for understanding one and the same christological title—notably, the title "Son of God," which early Christians sometimes predicated of Jesus primarily on the basis of Jewish assumptions typically made in using the term, while at other times their underlying assumptions in predicating it of him were not Jewish but Hellenistic and, therefore, very, very different, if they are taken simply as mythical or metaphysical claims about Jesus's being in himself. Consider, for example, the very different christologies expressed using this same title in the following three passages:

> Jesus Christ our Lord, declared to be Son of God with power according to the spirit of holiness by resurrection from the dead. (Rom 1:4)

> And just as he was coming up out of the water, he saw the heavens torn apart and the Spirit descending like a dove on him. And a voice came from heaven, "You are my Son, the Beloved, with you I am well pleased." (Mark 1:10–11)

> The angel said to her, "The Holy Spirit will come upon you, and the power of the Most High will overshadow you; therefore the child to be born will be holy; he will be called son of God." (Luke 1:35)

An even more fundamental distinction between one type of explicit christology and another (more fundamental because it cuts across the first distinction) is that between formulations that serve to explicate the christological assertion by ascribing one or another honorific title to Jesus (whether "the Christ" or "the Lord," "the Son of God," "the Son of Man," "the Word of God," or even, in later traditions, "God") and yet other formulations that explicate the assertion by means of what we today can think of only as mythological or legendary statements about Jesus's primal origin or final destiny or about the course of his life in between (such as statements about his miraculous conception and birth, his appointment to messianic office by his baptism, his resurrection from the dead, ascension into heaven, and session at the right hand of God). It may be worth pointing out in this connection that careful students of the Apostles' Creed such as J. N. D. Kelly have seen its second article as in effect combining these two different ways of explicitly making the christological assertion—the initial and presumably older formulation in terms of titles (according to which Jesus is the Christ, God's only Son, our Lord) being qualified by a whole series of relative clauses asserting Jesus's unique origin and destiny in God (such as that he was conceived by the Holy Spirit and born of the Virgin Mary and that on the third day he rose from the dead, ascended into heaven, and so on). Clearly, all such formulations, whether of the one kind or of the other, are logically of a piece in that they all serve to make one and the same christological assertion about Jesus's decisive significance for human existence.

4.1.3. Formal Analysis of the Christological Assertion

I cannot go into further detail about matters that are the proper concern, not of systematic theology, but of historical, and, specifically, biblical and New Testament theology. Instead, I must proceed to take the third and most important step in our consideration of the constitutive christological assertion and offer what I speak of as a proper *formal analysis* of it. As we have already noted, the christological assertion is like any other assertion in having a subject term and a predicate term so related by the copula as to assert the second, predicate term of the subject referred to by the first, subject term. In the case of this assertion, however, the striking thing, as we have seen, is that the subject term "Jesus" is constant throughout all formulations of the assertion—whether implicit or explicit, and whether in terms of honorific titles or mythical and legendary claims about the course of Jesus's life—while the predicate term, represented in the classical formulation by "the Christ," is variable, varying across the whole range of differences indicated by the distinctions just reviewed. Yet, however differently it may be formulated, the christological assertion is also like any other assertion in making or implying a claim to be true or credible, in the sense of being worthy of belief. In other words, any formulation of the assertion at least implicitly claims to tell the truth in asserting its variable predicate term, whatever it may be, of the referent of its constant subject term "Jesus." This implies, in turn, that the christological assertion is further like any other assertion that purports to be true in that, in any of its formulations, it is the answer to a question that first has to be understood if the assertion itself is to be understood and its distinctive claim to truth or credibility critically validated in an appropriate way.

Given these elementary observations about its grammatical and logical structure, it would appear that there are at least three questions that need to be asked and answered in order to proceed with a formal analysis of the christological assertion. In the logical order in which, in my judgment, they should be considered, these questions are:

1. To what question does the christological assertion provide the answer?

2. Who is the subject Jesus about whom the christological assertion is made?

3. What are the conditions that must be fulfilled if any christological predicate appropriately asserted of this subject is to be asserted of it credibly or truly?

The task now is to proceed with a formal analysis of the assertion by briefly answering these three questions. On this basis, we will then be in a position to go beyond all merely formal analysis to a constructive attempt to reformulate the material meaning of the assertion—in sec. 4.2, by attempting to determine the material identity of Jesus himself as attested by the formally normative witness of the apostles; and in sec. 4.3, by laying down the main lines of an adequate christology of liberation such as our situation today arguably makes desirable, if not, indeed, necessary.

It will be quickly recognized, I am sure, that the answers I shall give to the three questions are all controversial, being more or less sharply called into question by the very different answers that have in effect been given to them by other christologies, revisionary as well as classical. Because my concern here is primarily constructive, I shall not enter into the controversy concerning my answers and their alternatives as fully as I have elsewhere. My reader should realize, however, that, like practically everything else said here, or anywhere else on the same topics, what I shall say will open up not only the possibility but also the necessity of the reader's own theological reflection and decision—of making up her or his own mind about how the same questions should be answered if the resulting christology is to be both appropriate and credible. Obviously, if I did not think that my answers are relatively more adequate than any of the others that they exclude, I would not go to the trouble of setting them forth. But, on my understanding of what it means to be a theologian, answers are never as important as questions, and so my most important task, as I see it, is to be sure that the reader is given as good an idea as I am able to give of the full range of possible answers between which she or he will have to decide in the same way in which I, too, continually have to do.

I should probably say just a word about the distinction I regularly make and will also make in what follows between "*classical* christologies," on the one hand, and "*revisionary* christologies," on the other. By the first I mean all christologies conforming more or less closely to the christology formulated in the ancient church in the course of the controversies leading up to, and, in a way, settled by, the Council of Chalcedon in 451 CE. It was so-called Chalcedonian christology in this sense that was then substantially reaffirmed by both the Reformation and the Counter-Reformation, as well as, I may add, the later Wesleyan revival, and then systematized, refined, and further elaborated by the orthodox dogmatics of the late sixteenth through the eighteenth centuries. On the other hand, I mean by "revisionary christologies" the various attempts made by Friedrich Schleiermacher and many others from the late eighteenth century right up to the present to revise classical christologies more or less thoroughly. In so using the term, I deliberately intend to cover a wide variety of christologies—some of which have wanted to revise not merely by reformulating, but also by replacing, classical christologies (as in the case of probably most of the Protestant examples), while others (as in the case of most of the Roman Catholic ones) have not aimed to replace classical christologies, but only to reformulate them. I may add that I have provided a much fuller and, I trust, more adequate development of my answers to these three questions and the reasons therefor in my book, *The Point of Christology*.

To the logically first question, then, about the *question* to which the christological assertion gives an answer, I reply as follows: According to the answer that has usually been given to this question, in revisionary christologies as well as in classical ones, the question christology properly asks and answers is, "Who is Jesus?" understood as asking about the being of Jesus in himself, as distinct from asking about the meaning of Jesus for us. Thus, whether Jesus is understood with most classical christologies as uniquely *God in man*, God Godself uniquely present in and as a human being, or is understood, rather, with typically revisionary christologies, as uniquely *man of God*, a human being uniquely open to the gift and demand of God's love—in either case, the question to which the christological assertion is taken to be addressed is a question about the nature of

Jesus's person, his qualities, his mode of being, his relation to God, and so on. My contention, however, is that this answer, as widely prevalent as it has been both in the past and in the present, involves what Alfred North Whitehead cleverly dubs "the fallacy of misplaced concreteness." By this he means the fallacy that we always fall into whenever we treat what is really only an abstract part or aspect of some larger concrete whole as though it were that whole itself, or, at any rate, as though it were itself something concrete. To suppose, as practically all christologies have done and continue to do, that the only question the christological assertion answers is, "Who is Jesus?" is to commit this very fallacy, because it is to treat what is but one abstract aspect of the christological question as though it were the whole concrete question, or, at least, a concrete question logically independent of any of its other aspects.

I refer to what I call the "existential" aspects of the question, as distinct from its "historical" aspect, in which it certainly does have to do with the person or event named "Jesus." By the "existential aspects" of the question I mean the aspects that are disclosed by the variable predicate term of the christological assertion, whatever particular value of the variable may serve to formulate it. Thus, for example, if the predicate term of the assertion is "the Christ," the question the assertion answers is not only, "Who is Jesus?" but also, and even more fundamentally, "Who is the Christ?"

Further analysis discloses that the question of which "Who is the Christ?" is simply one particular formulation is what I have previously discussed as "the existential question," given, of course, the basic assumptions of a certain form of late Jewish religion contemporary with the rise of Christianity. It will be recalled from the discussion of God that it is this same existential question that I understand to be expressed in the question about God, given the presupposition of radical monotheism. As such, I argued, it is the universally human question that each woman and man unavoidably asks and answers simply by the fact of existing as a human being, whether or not she or he also asks and answers it explicitly, as the question about God, or in any other way, at the level of specific concepts and terms more or less appropriate for asking and answering it. It is, in short, our question simply as human beings about the meaning of ultimate reality for us, which, as I have already explained, is at one and the same time a question about ultimate reality, especially strictly ultimate reality, and a question about ourselves, about our authentic self-understanding, given what is ultimately real. Insofar as our existential question asks about ultimate reality, it has a *metaphysical* aspect in which it is closely related to, even while also being different from, the question of metaphysics proper. On the other hand, insofar as our question asks about our authentic self-understanding, about how we are authorized to understand ourselves and everything else by ultimate reality in its structure in itself, it also has a *moral* aspect in which it is both closely related to, and different from, the proper question of morality or ethics.

But, as I also pointed out earlier, it is typical of radical monotheism that the question about God is not the only way in which it asks the existential question about the meaning of ultimate reality for us. Once the concept-term "God" is accepted as appropriately applying to strictly ultimate reality—and just this, of course, is what radical monotheism in all its forms exists to make acceptable—the existential question no longer takes the form of asking, simply, "What is the meaning of *strictly ultimate reality* for us?" but asks, instead, "What is the meaning of *God* for us?" In this connection, then, radical monotheism, like other forms of theistic religion, typically generates yet another type or level of concepts and terms in which to think and speak about the meaning of God for us. Thus, in the tradition of the Hebrew scriptures and of the Judaism also assumed by the witness of the earliest Christian community, one speaks, for instance, of "the Spirit of God," "the Word of God," or "the Wisdom of God"—all ways of designating the meaning of God for us, as distinct from the being of God in itself. And in this connection, still other concepts and symbols emerge to designate anyone who, or anything that, represents God by making the meaning of God for us more or less fully explicit. Thus, in the same Jewish religious tradition, we find such concepts-terms as "prophet," "priest," and "king," each of which designates a figure who, in one way or another, re-presents God by somehow making the meaning of God for us explicit. The same is true of the concepts-symbols, "the Son of God," or "the Son of Man," or "the Messiah," although there may be some ambiguity about whether these concepts-terms primarily designate the meaning of God for us, as do "the Spirit of God," "the Word of God," or "the Wisdom of God," or rather primarily refer to historical figures, persons, or events that decisively re-present God's meaning so as to answer our question about God and to enable us to decide between all other putative re-presentations.

But, whatever the type or level of concepts-symbols in which it may be formulated—whether those referring to God, or to the meaning of God for us, or to those who re-present that meaning, or to one who re-presents it decisively—they all function religiously to provide the currency for explicitly asking and answering the existential question of the meaning of ultimate reality for us. And my point is that it is to this existential question that the christological assertion, in whatever formulation, also always gives an answer in answering the question, "Who is Jesus?" in its historical aspect. Accordingly, whether the predicate term of the assertion be "the Christ," or some other concept-symbol with which "the Christ" is functionally equivalent and interchangeable, the function of the predicate term when predicated of Jesus is to assert that precisely he decisively re-presents the meaning of God for us because he explicitly answers our existential question in both of its essential aspects, metaphysical and moral.

Thus, although the predicate term of the assertion does indeed always function to assert, in one way or another, who Jesus is—namely, the decisive re-presentation of the meaning of ultimate reality for us—at one and the same time, Jesus himself as the subject of the assertion always functions to interpret who "the Christ" is, or what is properly designated by any other appropriate and therefore functionally equivalent and interchangeable predicate term. So—to use again the example I used earlier in my discussion of God—when the Fourth Evangelist writes in the Prologue to his Gospel, "No one has ever seen God; the only Son, who is in the bosom of the Father, he has made God known," he evidently implies that Jesus is the only Son in the bosom of the Father (John 1:18; cf. 1:14). But the point of his assertion, clearly, is not only, or even most fundamentally, thus to identify Jesus purely *formally* as the only Son of God, but also and most fundamentally to identify the only true God *materially* as the Father whose only Son is Jesus, thereby authorizing an existence in obedient faith in *this* God as our authentic possibility as human beings.

Briefly, then, my answer to the first of our three questions is this: the question christology answers is not the simple question, "Who is Jesus?" but rather the complex question, "Who is Jesus? Who is the Christ? and so, Who is God? and Who am I?"—the latter three existential aspects of this complex question all being themselves aspects of the one existential question, which is fundamental to, because presupposed by, its first, historical aspect. This is why the historical question about Jesus to which the christological assertion gives the answer is not the *empirical-historical* question about the being of Jesus in himself then and there in the past,

66

but rather the *existential-historical* question about the meaning of Jesus) for us, here and now in the present.

But this is already to address the second of our three questions, which asks about the subject Jesus about whom the christological assertion is made. From what I have said, it should be clear that the Jesus who is the subject of the assertion is the historical person or event, even to be able to ask about which is possible only because of particular historical experience of just this person or event. True, this experience need not be immediate, as it was in the unique case of the earliest Christian witnesses, although it cannot fail to be at least mediate historical experience, in the sense of experience mediated by that of the first witnesses as well as of any of their successors through whom theirs has eventually come down to us. But if the Jesus who is the subject of the christological assertion is in this broad sense none other than "the Jesus of history," or "the historical Jesus," we still have to make a clear and sharp distinction between what I have just referred to as "the *empirical*-historical Jesus" and "the *existential*-historical Jesus." We must make this distinction because, as it happens, we can always be related not only to Jesus in particular but also to persons and events of the past in general in two very different ways: either empirically, in their being in themselves then and there in the past, or existentially, in their meaning for us here and now in the present.

By "the empirical-historical Jesus," then, I mean the historical reality that we are accustomed to refer to by the proper name, "Jesus," or "Jesus of Nazareth," considered in its being in itself then and there in the past insofar as we are able to know it today by way of empirical-historical inquiry. On the other hand, I mean by "the existential-historical Jesus" this same historical reality in its meaning for us here and now in the present insofar as we are able to know it through existential encounter with it, mediate if not immediate. I want to stress that, in both cases, we have to do with nothing other or less than the historical Jesus, or the Jesus of history, in the very broad, undifferentiated sense of these phrases. This is for the reason I already stated, namely, that we could not even ask about either the empirical-historical Jesus or the existential-historical Jesus, much less say anything at all by way of answering our question, except on the basis of a very particular historical experience of him—mediate if not immediate.

But because Jesus could not be experienced sufficiently to ask or answer either question apart from particular historical experience of him, we today, who are neither his immediate contemporaries nor any of their earlier successors, could not possibly have such experience except mediately through the experience of those who were. Since it is also only mediately, through their experience, that we can ever hope to answer either question, we must sooner or later have recourse to the witnesses borne by such immediate contemporaries, through which we alone have access to their experience. This means, for all practical purposes, that we must eventually recur to the earliest stratum of Christian witness to Jesus that we today are in a position to reconstruct.

I contend, however, that the function of this earliest stratum of witness is significantly different, depending on which of these two questions it is taken to answer. In being made to answer the empirical-historical question about the being of Jesus in himself, this witness is forced to function as a primary empirical-historical source, which it isn't. By contrast, in using it to answer the existential-historical question about the meaning of Jesus for us, we can allow this witness to function as the primary existential-historical authority that it intends to be and, in fact, is.

The upshot of all this is that my answer to our second question, determined as it must be by my answer to the first, is that the subject Jesus about whom the christological assertion is made is the existential-historical Jesus, not the empirical-historical Jesus. The assertion is not about the Jesus whom we are able to know only more or less probably through empirical-historical inquiry back behind the apostolic witness to him. Rather, the assertion is about the Jesus whom we are already able to know most certainly precisely through the apostles' witness, as well as, naturally, any other Christian witness that is authorized by theirs because or insofar as it substantially agrees with it.

Perhaps an analogy I have developed more fully elsewhere may help to make my point. It is the analogy suggested by the now classic discussion by H. Richard Niebuhr, in his book, *The Meaning of Revelation*, of the distinction between what he calls "external" and "internal" history—a distinction, by the way, that I take to be closely parallel to mine between "empirical-historical" and "existential-historical" ways of relating to the past. Niebuhr contrasts two very different references to the same event of 4 July 1776: the one, the description of the event given by a contemporary British historian in the *Cambridge Modern History;* the other, the obvious allusion to this event made by Abraham Lincoln in the opening words of his Gettysburg Address. The significance of this example for our purposes is to clarify what an American patriot like Lincoln means in speaking of the event that was the origin of his nation. Clearly, he means nothing other or less than an actual historical happening, prior to and distinct from both his own patriotic devotion and that of all other American patriots who have preceded him, right back to the founding fathers themselves. And yet it is just as clear that the only event the patriot means to refer to is the existential-historical event that, in originating the American nation, is the primal authorizing source of his own and all other American patriotism that is at all appropriate. This is why the whole meaning of the event, as Lincoln refers to it, is summed up by identifying it simply as the bringing forth of "a new nation, conceived in liberty, and dedicated to the proposition that all men are created equal." Whatever may in fact have happened, as empirical-historical research might be able to establish it, the only thing about the event that is of interest to Lincoln or to any other American patriot for whom he speaks is that it is the origin of a nation so conceived and so dedicated, and hence the primal authorizing source of their own as well as of all other authentic Americanism.

Analogously, I should say, the event that the New Testament witnesses mean in referring to Jesus does, indeed, belong to the origin of the church of which they are members, and so is an actual happening, prior to and independent of not only their own faith and witness, but even of the faith and witness of the apostles who are its founders. But there is the further analogy that, in this case, too, the whole meaning of the event, so far as the New Testament is concerned, is expressed in formulations that, in one conceptuality and terminology or another, represent it as the existential-historical event that is at once the decisive revelation of God and the primal authorizing source of all that is appropriately Christian. This is why the referent of the name "Jesus" in any such formulation as "Jesus is the Christ" is not at all someone whom we first come to know only more or less probably by empirical-historical inquiry back behind the witness of the apostles as well as the later witnesses who authored the New Testament writings. Rather, "Jesus" refers to the one whom we are already given to know most certainly through the same apostolic witness as well as all other witnesses of faith, in the New Testament and after it, insofar as they are conformed to the formally normative witness of the apostles.

This leaves our third question about the conditions that must be fulfilled if any christological predicate appropriately asserted of Jesus is also to be asserted of him credibly or truly. According to the classical answer to this question Jesus can be truly said to be the Christ, or any of the other things that Christians appropriately assert him to be, if, and only if, in his own being in himself, he is somehow uniquely *God in man*, which is to say, God Godself uniquely present somehow in and as a human being. By contrast, modern revisionary christologies have typically answered this question by claiming that Jesus can be truly asserted to be the Christ if, and only if, in his own being in himself, he is uniquely *man of God*, which is to say, a human being somehow uniquely open to God, whether by being uniquely conscious of God, faithful to God, obedient to God, or what have you. But for all of the differences between these two main types of answers, they are, as I pointed out earlier, essentially the same insofar as they presuppose the same question about the being of Jesus in himself, which they take to be the proper question of christology. In my view, on the contrary, this is precisely *not* the christological question, which asks, rather, as I have argued, about the meaning of Jesus for us, by which I mean, of course, for all of us as human beings, not merely for us as Christians.

Because it is this very different question that christology asks and answers, the conditions that must be fulfilled by any true answer to it must be correspondingly different. I maintain, therefore, that Jesus can be truly asserted to be the Christ, or any of the other things that Christians appropriately assert or imply him to be, if, and only if, the possibility of self-understanding that he explicitly authorizes as the authentic understanding of ourselves in relation to ultimate reality is, in truth, our authentic self-understanding—which is to say, is, in truth, the self-understanding that is always already authorized at least implicitly by our existence as such, through all our experience and reason simply as human beings of the meaning of ultimate reality for us! Thus, in my view, Jesus really and truly is who the christological assertion asserts him to be—namely, the decisive re-presentation of the meaning of ultimate reality for us—if, and only if, in his meaning for us, he explicitly authorizes us to exist as we are implicitly called to exist by all our experience as human beings, regardless of whether, in his being in himself, he is or is not either somehow uniquely God in man or somehow uniquely man of God.

4.2. JESUS WHO IS SAID TO BE THE CHRIST

So much for what I have called a *formal analysis* of the christological assertion. I turn now to the other important task of setting forth what I understand to be a *material interpretation* of it. To this end, I want to consider the material identity of the subject of the assertion—of who, exactly, Jesus himself is. Precisely because the point of the christological assertion is most fundamentally an éxistential point, the question of the subject of the assertion, of his material identity, is the absolutely crucial question. Literally everything depends on determining just who Jesus is; for it is precisely and only Jesus who gives what is otherwise a purely formal claim about his decisive significance for human existence, and therefore about the meaning of ultimate reality for us, its distinctive material meaning. Of course, my answer to the question of who Jesus is materially is already on record. I could not have said any of the things I have said about God, creation, and human existence—or, for that matter, even about theology itself—without assuming an answer to it. But, as I have explained already, my responsibility now is to argue *for* what I have hitherto simply assumed and argued *from*. I need to make good on my claim that Charles Wesley got it exactly right when he confessed, in the words of "Love Divine, All Loves Excelling": "Jesus, thou art all compassion, pure, unbounded love thou art."

I would recall two theses that will be familiar from what I have already said in this or earlier discussions: (1) that the Jesus who is the subject of the christological assertion is the existential-historical Jesus, as distinct from the empirical-historical Jesus; and (2) that the formally normative witness by which the appropriateness of all other Christian witness to Jesus is to be judged is the original and originating and therefore constitutive witness of the apostles. So far as we today are concerned, this means, not the New Testament canon as such, but rather "the canon *before* the canon" in the earliest stratum of Christian witness that we are now in a position to reconstruct, using the extant New Testament writings as sources and employing our own best historical methods and knowledge. If these two theses are correct, then Jesus who is said to be the Christ is the existential-historical Jesus attested by the earliest stratum of the synoptic tradition, which is to say, the tradition concerning Jesus that lies behind, and is redacted in, the extant synoptic gospels.

Following one of the leading students of this earliest stratum of Jesus-tradition, Willi Marxsen, I speak of it as "Jesus-kerygma," because, although the individual units in which it consists are precisely Christian witness to Jesus in the form of kerygma or proclamation, instead of historical reportage, they are nonetheless proclamation of *Jesus*, not of Christ, or even of Jesus Christ. In other words, theirs is an *implicit* christology only, not an explicit christology, as was presumably true also of Jesus's own christology if, or insofar as, his proclamation included any such. Our question, then, about the material meaning of Jesus Christ, or—in the words of the New Testament—of "Jesus who is said to be the Christ," is, finally, the question about the Jesus attested by the Jesus-kerygma.

Students of the Jesus-kerygma widely agree that its religious presuppositions are those of late Jewish apocalypticism, with its characteristically dual, though hardly dualistic, world view distinguishing between two ages: the present evil age of the world, understood to be now approaching its end; and the new age that God is soon to bring about as at once the judgment and the fulfillment of the present age, thereby redeeming God's promise to Israel, by which it has long been sustained and to which, as God's chosen people, it has been called to bear witness. The distinctive thing about the Jesus-kerygma, however, is its witness to *Jesus himself* as the decisive act by which the coming new age of God has already begun. Through the person or event of Jesus of Nazareth, God has already acted in a definitive way to call together from out of its dispersion the congregation of the last days, the new Israel of the saints and the elect, who are already to live out of God's future here and now in the present.

The point of the Jesus-kerygma in thus bearing witness to Jesus is, of course, to summon others to make the decision that Jesus means also for themselves, even as for those who, having already made it by "following" Jesus, are now proclaiming him. But the distinctive thing about their kerygma, which explains calling it, precisely, "*Jesus*-kerygma," is that it proclaims Jesus himself as God's decisive act, as God's own call to decision, only implicitly, by representing Jesus as himself the proclaimer of God's imminent reign or rule. As such, Jesus claims a decisive significance for the sheer fact of his proclamation that already confronts his hearers with the decision between continuing to live simply in the old age and daring to live already in God's new age even though still remaining in the old one. Thus, according to the stylized summary at the beginning of the Gospel of Mark, "After John [*sc.* the Baptist] was arrested, Jesus came into Galilee, preaching the gospel of God, and saying, 'The time is fulfilled, and the rule of God is at hand; repent and believe the gospel'" (Mark 1:14–15).

Many historical-critical students of Christian origins agree that, in all probability, Jesus did in fact appear on the scene as an apocalyptic prophet and teacher with just such a proclamation: on the one hand, of the imminent coming of God's rule, and, on the other, of the possibility and necessity of his hearers even now turning their lives around and already understanding themselves in terms of the good news of God's coming reign. But whether or not the empirical-historical Jesus was in fact the kind of apocalyptic prophet and teacher that the Jesus-kerygma represents him as being, the point of the Jesus-kerygma, no less than that of the later Christ-kerygma and Jesus-Christ-kerygma, with their more explicit christologies, is to witness to Jesus himself as of decisive significance for any hearer of the kerygma, even as for those now proclaiming it. Precisely through Jesus himself, in and through all that he said and did, as prophet and teacher, God Godself has already acted so as to confront anyone who encounters him with God's own gift and demand—either immediately, as in the case of the disciples, or mediately, through the disciples-now-become-apostles' own experience and witness.

But just what, materially speaking, are God's gift and demand as they are decisively re-presented through Jesus himself? They are, in a word, the gift and demand of love, of a boundless love that authorizes—i.e., both entitles and empowers—a human existence of obedient faith working through love and love incarnating itself as justice. Thus, according to the Jesus-kerygma, Jesus himself, through everything that he says and does, *means love*—both God's prevenient love for all of us and, on this basis, through our obedient faith in God's love, our own returning love for God and for all whom God loves.

Here, again, most students of the traditions comprising the Jesus-kerygma who are concerned with Christian origins infer from their witness not only that Jesus *means* love but also that Jesus *meant* love. They infer, in other words, that the empirical-historical Jesus himself did in fact intend, through all that he said and did, to confront all with whom he had to do with the fact of God's love for each of them and with their own possibility as individual persons so to entrust themselves to God's love as to be faithful to its cause and to lead their own lives as lives of love. In my view, everything speaks for this empirical-historical inference, and nothing speaks against it, beyond, naturally, the difficulty in principle of inferring what Jesus intended, or, for that matter, what he said and did, solely from what are at best secondary empirical-historical sources uncontrolled and uncontrollable by any primary ones. But whatever may or may not have been the case with the empirical-historical Jesus, whether he *meant* love in this sense or not, the existential-historical Jesus proclaimed by the Jesus-kerygma is proclaimed as the one who *means* love, not only for his contemporaries or for those who proclaim him, but also for all to whom their proclamation continues to be addressed. Through Jesus himself, they assert, God's own love continues to be decisively re-presented as the gift and demand that authorizes us to exist in obedient faith in God and in love both for God and for all whom God loves.

Once again, however, I stress that the distinctive thing about the Jesus-kerygma is that it makes this assertion about Jesus only implicitly—not through *what* it says about him explicitly, but through the fact *that* what it says about him is said precisely *as kerygma*, as witness of faith in the double sense that it arises out of the decision of faith of those who bear it and that it then calls for the same decision of faith from those to whom it is borne.

But if the Jesus-kerygma does not make the christological assertion explicitly as such but only implies this assertion, it nonetheless enables us to understand what any formulation of the assertion would have to assert, in some terms or other, in order to make explicit what it as Jesus-kerygma very definitely implies—by its *that*, if not in its *what*. If any explicit formulation of the assertion is to be valid, in the sense that it is appropriate to Jesus Christ because it agrees in substance with the formally normative witness of the apostles—if any such formulation is to be valid, what it explicitly asserts is that the Jesus who means love is the decisive re-presentation of the meaning of God for us and that, therefore, the meaning of strictly ultimate reality for us is nothing other or less than the "all compassion, the pure, unbounded love" that Jesus himself means.

It is just this, however, that I judge to be more or less appropriately asserted, in one way or another, by all of the several different explicit christologies that we find in the New Testament. Whether only or primarily in the terms of late Jewish religious tradition, apocalypticist or otherwise, or rather in the terms of one or the other of the non-Jewish religious traditions present in the Greek-speaking ecumene, such as Gnosticism or the mystery religions, say, the various more or less explicit christologies that we find in the New Testament writings are but so many different ways of formulating or reformulating this basic assertion that is already clearly implied by the Jesus-kerygma of the apostles.

This seems to me to be true, notably, of the christology of the cross and resurrection that evidently began to develop quite early, since there are clear indications of it already prior to Paul, even if it is in his letters that it is first given its classic interpretation. For this particular form of Christ-kerygma, it is Jesus's crucifixion and resurrection by the power of God that are taken to be the saving event, the event of God's liberating judgment of the world, through which all who are willing to die with Christ are given to rise with him to newness of life. What is striking to the New Testament historian, however, is that this whole explicit christology is all but completely missing in the earliest stratum of Christian witness constituting the implicit christology of the Jesus-kerygma. In the Jesus-kerygma, the saving event is not at all Jesus's death and resurrection, but Jesus's proclamation or witness, in its *that* as distinct from its *what*—in the *event* of his proclaiming or bearing it and of his hearers being confronted with its offer. It is *this* event, which happens in and through all that Jesus says and does, that the synoptic tradition generally takes to be the saving event—with the result that there are only two passages in this entire tradition in which Jesus is represented as speaking of his death as the event of salvation (one being the passage in which he speaks of his life as a "ransom" [Mark 10:45], the other being his saying in connection with the last supper [Mark 14:22–24]); and both of these passages are evidently relatively late, having originated, not in the earliest Palestinian community, but in the later Hellenistic church. Also striking is that the hypothetical sayings source Q has nothing at all to say about either the cross or the resurrection as saving event.

Of course, as Marxsen has argued, the fact that the Jesus-kerygma continued to be proclaimed *as kerygma* even after Jesus's death is implicit witness to his resurrection, in that he was experienced by the disciples as alive after his death and, notwithstanding his crucifixion, as still decisively re-presenting God's love and authorizing their obedient trust in it and loyalty to it. But the fact remains that the Jesus-kerygma knows nothing of the explicit christology of cross and resurrection and that, for this reason, such a christology is, in fact, itself already a reformulation of the apostolic witness, and one that, on the face of it, might well have been suspected of teaching "another gospel" than that originally taught by the apostles themselves.

And this, I may add, is just why I am completely unwilling to privilege the explicit christology of cross and resurrection—or, if you will, of Good Friday, Easter, and Pentecost—as *the* New Testament kerygma. As much as I agree that the still later explicit christologies of the infancy narratives or of the ascension, say, must be referred back to something more fundamental than themselves by reference to which their meaning is to be understood and their validity validated as appropriate Christian witness, I fundamentally disagree that what they must be referred back to is the explicit christology of crucifixion and resurrection. *This* christology is not the christology that norms (*christologia normans*), but rather one of the christologies that *is to be normed* (*christologia normanda*)—namely, by the implicit christology of the apostles, i.e., the Jesus-kerygma attested by the earliest stratum of the synoptic tradition.

Still and all, I am convinced that the only point that Paul, at any rate, is concerned to make by his christology of cross and resurrection is substantially the same point that the apostles themselves were concerned to make by their merely implicit christology. By representing Jesus's cross and resurrection as God's liberating judgment of the world—or, as he can also put it, as God's reconciliation of the world to Godself (2 Cor 5:18ff.)—Paul wants to say nothing other than that Jesus means love, that he himself is the decisive re-presentation of God's love for us, which explicitly authorizes, i.e., both entitles and empowers, our own obedient faith working through love.

I cannot further argue this important point—by showing, for example, that other New Testament christologies for which the decisive saving event is Jesus's birth or his adoption by God at his baptism are also but functionally equivalent and interchangeable ways of making one and the same existential point. I must be content simply to summarize my argument by saying that the Jesus who is said to be the Christ is the decisive re-presentation of God's love and that, for all of the differences in the terms in which they formulate this assertion, both between themselves and between all of them and the merely implicit christology of the Jesus-kerygma, the explicit christologies of the New Testament are arguably all more or less appropriate ways of saying precisely this, given the assumptions of the different historical situations in and for which they sought to formulate it.

4.3. FOR FREEDOM CHRIST HAS SET US FREE

If the preceding section has succeeded in what it was concerned to do, the reader should now have at least some understanding of why I have taken the material meaning of Jesus Christ to be the decisive re-presentation of God's love as the gift and demand of our own existence in obedient faith working through love. But, then, it should also be clear how, in my opinion, one would have to go about validating the appropriateness of any contemporary constructive christology. If any christology developed in and for our situation today is to be appropriate to Jesus Christ because it is in substantial agreement with the formally normative witness of the apostles, it will somehow have to interpret and reformulate the assertion that the Jesus who means love is the decisive re-presentation of the meaning of God for us—which is to say, of the meaning of strictly ultimate reality for us.

One of the ways, certainly, in which just such a contemporary christology may well be developed is to work out an adequate christology of liberation. Considering the importance of the question of liberation or emancipation for all sorts and conditions of human beings today, one can readily understand why a number of Christian thinkers have concerned themselves with such a project. To represent Jesus himself as the Liberator and the salvation he re-presents as liberation is to speak in terms in which many persons today commonly think and speak in asking and answering their existential question as human beings. But the question naturally arises whether this way of thinking and speaking is, after all, also appropriate to Jesus Christ because it is also in substantial agreement with the merely implicit and yet formally normative witness of the apostles.

I contend that it is thus appropriate, provided, at least, that what is meant by "Liberator" and "liberation" is rightly understood. If Jesus who is said to be the Christ is the Jesus who means love—God's prevenient love for us and therefore the possibility of our returning love for God and for all whom God loves—if this is who Jesus is rightly understood to be, then one can certainly say that Jesus also means *freedom*. This is so, at any rate, insofar as one is willing to recognize that to exist in obedient faith in God's prevenient love for us and in returning love for God and for neighbor as self in God is to exist precisely in radical freedom—both freedom *from* and freedom *for* oneself and all of one's fellow creatures. Because God's love for us is utterly boundless and is freely offered to any-

and everyone who will but receive it, nothing whatever can ever separate any of us from life's ultimate meaning. For this reason, to accept God's love through obedient faith is to be freed *from* oneself and everything else as in any way a necessary condition of an ultimately meaningful life. "Let goods and kindred go,/ this mortal life also;/ the body they may kill;/ God's truth abideth still;/ his kingdom is forever." But, for the very same reason, the acceptance of God's love through obedient faith establishes one's freedom *for* all things as well as one's freedom from them. Because God's love is utterly boundless and embraces everyone and everything within its scope, anyone and anything whatever is of ultimate significance *in* God and thus is the proper object of one's returning love *for* God.

In the case of other persons such as oneself, one can be thus free for them only by furthering their own freedom to be and to become themselves—acting subjects or agents of their own self-creation, instead of merely passive objects or victims of the self-creations of others. In this sense, the existence of obedient faith whose possibility is decisively re-presented through Jesus is a *liberating* as well as a *liberated* existence; it is an existence *for* the freedom of oneself and all others as well as an existence *in* the freedom that is the gift and demand of God's love.

Because this is so, the project of a christology of liberation seems to me to be eminently appropriate. Provided that what one means by "liberation" is the existence of radical freedom established through obedient faith in God's love; and that what one means by "the Liberator" is the one through whom just such an existence of freedom is decisively authorized, there seems to me no question that the christology implied by the Jesus-kerygma is substantially, even if not formally, a christology of liberation. For the Jesus to whom it bears witness is the one through whom just such an existence of radical freedom is decisively re-presented.

But is *this* "christology of liberation" what is properly meant by the concept today? Isn't the christology of liberation for whose appropriateness I have just been arguing simply the kind of christology of liberation that Paul and John already projected, in their ways, in New Testament times? And hasn't it long been made clear that what they meant by "freedom" is *not* what is meant by the term "liberation" and its cognates as it is widely used today in Christian witness and theology?

The point is well taken. So far as I am concerned, at any rate, the christology of liberation whose outlines I have sketched is substantially, if not formally, very much the christology that Paul presupposes in Galatians or that John implies in the eighth chapter of his gospel. But I maintain—and have argued at length in the last chapter of *The Point of Christology*—that existence *in* freedom in this specifically Christian meaning of the words necessarily implies an existence *for* freedom also in its contemporary secular meaning of social, cultural, economic, and political freedom.

My argument, briefly, is that faith, by its very nature, works through love and that love, in turn, always incarnates itself in justice, which is to say, in giving to each person her or his own (*suum cuique*). This love does by taking account of each person's needs and then acting to meet these needs, so far as it is possible to do so. But whatever may have been true of earlier generations, we today know that the achievement of justice in this sense cannot be confined simply to acting *within* established social and cultural orders. Because these orders themselves are one and all human creations, the products of human decisions rather than decisions either of nature or of nature's God, human beings also bear the responsibility for maintaining the orders already established by their forebears or, whenever necessary, for improving them and even transforming them. Insofar as established structures of social and cultural order serve to realize the ends for which they are created, they deserve to be maintained so that they can continue to serve these ends. But insofar as such structures stand in the way of realizing their proper ends, they need either to be improved so that they will serve their ends, or else to be transformed—perhaps, even radically. But all of this work of maintaining and improving or transforming social and cultural structures is included in our responsibility to achieve justice, which itself is necessarily implied by the fundamental demand of love. Consequently, as different as Christian freedom certainly is from any and all forms of secular freedom, to exist in Christian freedom by existing in faith working through love and love incarnating itself in justice is to exist for the realization of secular freedom, also, in all of its relevant forms.

But, then, the christology of liberation that I have suggested has as much claim to the title as any other. Indeed, it has a much stronger claim insofar as its concern for securing secular freedom, and thus for emancipation in all its forms, is not taken over from elsewhere and simply imposed on Christian faith and life, but is firmly grounded in the very freedom for which Christ has set us free. But if, for this reason, it has a clear title to be called a *christology* of liberation, its inclusion of existence for secular freedom as integral to existence in faith itself also entitles it to be called a christology *of liberation*—not in any merely abstract, ethereal, or otherworldly sense of the words, but in the concrete, down-to-earth, this-worldly sense of existing in solidarity with all who are oppressed and of acting to emancipate them from their oppression.

5

On the Holy Spirit

5.1. DO WE NEED "A THEOLOGY OF THE HOLY SPIRIT"?

BEING A CHRISTIAN IN the United Methodist tradition, I have often heard the claim, expressed or implied, that its theologians have a particular reason to be concerned with the theology of the Holy Spirit—indeed, that their distinctive contribution to ecumenical theology should take the form, above all, of developing such a theology. I, for one, however, seriously question the validity of this claim. If it is true, as I believe it is, that even for a United Methodist Christian *as theologian*, the task of Christian systematic theology has nothing peculiarly to do with what United Methodists have traditionally believed and borne witness to, any more than with the traditional beliefs and witnesses of Christians generally—if this is true, then there is no more reason for United Methodists who are theologians than for any other Christian theologians to be concerned with developing a theology of the Holy Spirit.

Furthermore, in John Wesley's case at least, the person and work of the Holy Spirit are by no means singled out for particular theological treatment, nor does the important role that he admittedly assigns the Spirit necessarily call for such treatment. Striking in Wesley's own theology, on the contrary, are the balanced *trinitarian* formulations in which it abounds. Thus, in his sermon, "The Scripture Way of Salvation," for example, it is not peculiarly the Spirit to whom he assigns the divine working in the soul that is vulgarly called "natural conscience" (but that, on his view is properly termed "preventing grace"); rather, it is *the entire trinity*. Accordingly, he elaborates what he means by "preventing grace" by speaking of

> . . . all the "drawings" of "the Father," the desires after God, which, if we yield to them, increase more and more; all that "light" where-

with the Son of God "enlighteneth everyone that cometh into the world," *showing* every man "to do justly, to love mercy, and to walk humbly with his God"; all the *convictions* which his Spirit from time to time works in every child of man. Although it is true the generality of men stifle them as soon as possible, and after a while forget, or at least deny, that ever they had them at all.[1]

The conspicuous absence from this formulation of the coordinating conjunction "and" between (1) "the drawings of the Father"; (2) the light wherewith the Son enlightens; and (3) the convictions of the Spirit, warrants our taking Wesley to intend them as simply three different ways— none more apt or important than the other—of speaking of the one work of the triune God *ad extra* that is God's prevenient grace.

But the more important point I would call attention to is the curious place that the doctrine of the Holy Spirit has held down through the whole history of Christian witness and theology. It is well known that the full deity of the Spirit was not clearly asserted until well after that of the Son had been dogmatically defined—and even the final version of the Apostles' Creed is striking in its simple, undeveloped confession, "I believe in the Holy Spirit," which leaves the precise identity and function of the Spirit, to say nothing of the Spirit's coequality with the Father and the Son, quite undefined (although one could well urge that the other things confessed in the third article—"I believe in . . . the holy catholic church, the communion of saints, the forgiveness of sins, the resurrection of the body, and the live everlasting"—all imply a number of important assertions concerning the Spirit's person and work). Furthermore, in many, if not most, theological appropriations of the Christian witness, the significance of the Holy Spirit has as a rule been explicated not by devoting a particular chapter to it—as I am doing here—but by explicating it in each of the several other chapters where it is relevant.

Thus the Holy Spirit is typically dealt with in orthodox dogmatics in the chapter, "On Sacred Scripture," in connection with the doctrines of the inspiration of scripture and of the "internal testimony of the Holy Spirit" (*testimonium spiritus sancti internum*). Or, again, it is dealt with in the chapter "On God," specifically in the section, "*De Deo Trino*," in the doctrines of "the procession of the Holy Spirit from the Father and the Son" and of the "internal" works of the trinity—generation and spiration—and

---

1. Outler, ed., *The Works of John Wesley*, vol. 2: *Sermons II*, 156–57.

its "external" works—creation, redemption, and sanctification. In the chapter, "On Christ," also, the Spirit has traditionally been considered in connection with the doctrines of Christ's miraculous conception by the Holy Spirit and of his reception of the Spirit at his baptism. Then, in the doctrine of salvation, the Spirit has been treated by defining salvation as "the applied power (or grace) of the Holy Spirit," while in ecclesiology, the Spirit appears in connection both with the doctrine of the origin of the church at Pentecost, and with the doctrine of the nature of the church as *communio sanctorum* (communion of saints or holy persons and/or of holy things). Finally, the significance of the Spirit has also been explicated in the chapter, "On the Last Things," especially in connection with the doctrine of the final outpouring of the Spirit on all flesh (Acts 2:17–21).

If this sketch of the several ways in which the Spirit has been thought and spoken about in orthodox theology attests to the comprehensive significance of the Spirit for the Christian understanding of human existence, it also makes clear that it is hardly necessary to devote a particular chapter to the Spirit in order to give adequate expression to such significance—assuming, at any rate, that the traditional treatment of the Spirit, given its characteristic presuppositions and limitations, is by no means inadequate. The pertinence of this point to the argument here is to underscore further what has already been said or implied more than once, that there is no Platonic idea of the perfect Christian theology, of which any theology that is to be at all responsible or adequate must be an imitation. *How* one deals with the Holy Spirit—even, perhaps, *whether* one develops any separate doctrine of the Spirit at all—is something that, judging from the entire history of Christian witness and theology, one has both the freedom and the responsibility to decide, given one's own understanding of the understanding of Christian faith.

But, for better or worse, my own freedom and responsibility in this respect have been preempted by my decision to devote a separate discussion to the Holy Spirit in the understanding of Christian faith I am outlining here. Accordingly, in what follows, I shall first comment rather generally on the relation between an understanding of the Holy Spirit and specifically Christian faith and experience; I shall then set forth summarily the doctrine I should wish to develop concerning the person and work of the Holy Spirit; finally, I shall indicate briefly what I understand by "life in the Spirit," or "according to the Spirit," concluding with some remarks about what it means to live such a life insofar as one has the special vocation to be a representative minister of the church and therefore also a professional theologian.

5.2. THE HOLY SPIRIT IN CHRISTIAN FAITH AND EXPERIENCE

The American New Testament theologian, John Knox, has made two statements that I have long found it fruitful to ponder together. There is, first, his statement that

> the sole residuum of the event [*sc.* of Christ] was the church. The only difference between the world as it was just after the event and the world as it had been just before is that the church was now in existence. A new kind of human community had emerged; a new society had come into being. There was absolutely nothing besides. This new community held and prized vivid memories of the event in which it had begun. It had a new faith; that is, it saw the nature of the world and of God in a new light. It found in its own life the grounds—indeed, anticipatory fulfillments—of a magnificent hope. But the memory, the faith, and the hope were all its own; they had neither existence nor ground outside of the community. Only the church really existed. Except for the church the event had not occurred.[2]

This is no doubt a provocative statement of Knox's point, some of whose formulations one might well wish to question. Yet I cannot but think that he says something absolutely essential to an understanding of Christianity as a historical reality as well as to any adequate theological understanding of Christian existence. From a historical standpoint, it can be said without risk of contradiction that "the sole residuum of the event [of Christ] was the church"—understanding, of course, that the church, in turn, then left its mark on a much wider history in all kinds of direct and indirect ways. Although the church has always understood itself as the response to an event prior to it and independent of it, it has also claimed—and with justification—that the only access to this event is in and through its own life and witness. Thus, in the faith and experience of individual Christians, it is always and only in and through the church that they have any share in the event of Jesus Christ, which is not only the origin of the church in history but the very principle of its existence as

2. Knox, *The Early Church and the Coming Great Church*, 45.

the church. The church continues to exist *as* the church only because, or insofar as, it is the community of believing and witnessing response to the event of Jesus Christ. And yet no Christian who understands the conditions of her or his own existence can ever think of playing the event off against the church in such a way as to imply that the church is somehow unimportant. And this is so, regardless of the judgments that she or he may make, and even find it necessary to make, about some one or more of the institutional churches. As critical as we may and must always be of all the Christian churches, our own included, the only ground of the appropriateness of our criticism—because the only source of its criterion—is the church itself as the community of believing and witnessing response to the decisive event of Jesus Christ.

In another passage in the same book, however, Knox makes a rather different statement:

> [T]he early church not only shared in a common memory; it also participated in a common Spirit . . . [T]he two belong inseparably together. If the event had not been remembered, the Spirit could not have come; but without the Spirit, the event could not have been remembered just as it was remembered, for the reason that it could not have happened just as it did happen. For the event was, in its final issue, the coming of the Spirit. Only those who had received the Spirit could really remember the event, for it was only to them that the event had really occurred.[3]

Whereas in the first statement we considered, Knox says that it was "the church" that was the "sole residuum" of the event, he says here that the "final issue" of the event was "the coming of the Spirit." The significance of this apparent, but, I believe, only apparent, contradiction is that the second statement is by way of saying *theologically* what the first says, primarily, *historically.*

It is distinctive of Christian faith and experience, as I understand them, to think and speak of the church as precisely the community of the Spirit—even as what Christians think and speak of as the Spirit is the empowering presence whose continuing work occurs explicitly and decisively in and through the community of the church. The church, as we shall see in greater detail hereafter, is the community that first came into being as a visible community with the explicit coming of the Spirit and

3. Ibid., 55–56.

in which the event of Jesus Christ that constitutes that community ever continues to take place through the Spirit's own witness to it. Thus the very existence of the church as the community of obedient faith responding to God's decisive self-revelation through Jesus is the gift of the Spirit of God; and so, in encountering the church, as Christians do, as the immediate ground of their own Christian faith and witness, they cannot but understand this encounter as itself an encounter with God—with God's own Holy Spirit. Even as the church is the community that the Spirit of God calls into being, so the historical community that is the church is adequately understood theologically only as the visible, audible presence of the Spirit of God. As Irenæus put it toward the end of the second century CE, "where the church is, there is the Spirit of God, and where the Spirit of God is, there is the church and all grace"—to which I would add only that there is an *implicit* as well as an explicit presence of the church, just as there is an *implicit* as well as an explicit presence of the Holy Spirit.

So much, then, by way of general comment on the relation of the Christian understanding of the Holy Spirit to specifically Christian faith and experience. The point I have been concerned to make is twofold: (1) that the church as the visible community of witness to Jesus Christ participates in the primary authority of the apostles that explicitly authorizes all specifically Christian faith and experience; and (2) that the primal source of such faith and experience as well as of the church's authority in explicitly authorizing it essentially involves what Christians understand by "the Holy Spirit"—just as surely as it essentially involves what they mean by "Jesus Christ."

5.3. THE LORD, THE GIVER OF LIFE

But how is it, exactly, that the Holy Spirit is essentially involved in the primal source of the faith and experience of Christians who, as such, are members of the community called church? I will answer this question by offering a summary statement of the doctrine of the Holy Spirit as I think it should be developed. Although the Apostles' Creed, as I remarked earlier, is notably inexplicit about just who the Holy Spirit is and what the Holy Spirit does, we know from the more explicit formulations of the so-called Nicene Creed who the Spirit had long been understood to be, indeed, from New Testament times on—namely, "the Lord, the giver of life." By "the Holy Spirit," Christians have commonly understood God as the giver of life—the One who, in the beginning, gives us our life as creatures, and hence the primal source of our *existence as such*, as well as, and above all, the One who, in the end, gives us *new* life, and hence is the primal source of *authentic existence* in obedient faith working through love. Thus we may say (to put the essence of the matter in a single thesis): the Holy Spirit is the empowering presence of God Godself as the only primal source of authentic faith and love even as of our very existence as creatures.

The basic point here may seem less mysterious or recondite if we simply reflect for a moment on how it is that we in fact come to put our faith or trust in another human person. I submit that where our trust in another is real, we are always more or less conscious of the fact that it is nothing we owe to ourselves, even though our act of trust is certainly our own free and responsible act. Rather, our trust is something quite literally called forth in us by the empowering presence of the other person disclosing her- or himself to us as faithful and therefore, as we say, trustworthy. In short, even in our ordinary human relations, our trust in another person—and the same could be said, I think, of our loyalty to, or love for another—is a gift, something that we owe, not to ourselves, but precisely to the other.

So it is, also, by analogy, with trust in God and loyalty to God, or, in other words, obedient faith in God and returning love for God as well as for all whom God loves. What Christian witness and theology properly mean by the Holy Spirit is precisely God as the primal source whose presence *empowers* our authentic existence as well as our existence as such, just as what they properly mean by the Son of God incarnate in Jesus Christ is that same primal source insofar as it *entitles* us thus to exist in authentic faith and love.

I am here recalling, of course, my earlier discussion of the doctrine of the trinity, where I accepted the conventional distinction between the "economic trinity," or "trinity of revelation," on the one hand, and the "ontological trinity," "essential trinity," or "immanent trinity," on the other. Given this distinction, I explained the economic trinity, or trinity of revelation, as follows: God is revealed through Jesus Christ as the primal source authorizing our authentic existence, where "to authorize" is assumed to mean both *to entitle*, or to give us the *right* to, and *to empower*, by giving us the *power* to, understand ourselves authentically. Considered, then, simply as *the primal source* that authorizes our authentic existence,

God is revealed as the Father; considered as the primal source *entitling* us, or giving us the right, so to understand ourselves, God is revealed as the Son; and considered as the primal source *empowering* us, or giving us the power, so to understand ourselves, God is revealed as the Holy Spirit.

But, then, the economic trinity, or trinity of revelation, in this sense implies as the necessary condition of its possibility the ontological, essential, or immanent trinity, i.e., the trinity that God must be simply as such or in Godself in order to be, as Christians believe, the primal source of our authentic existence. Provided that the primal source of our authenticity is none other than God as God is and must be in order to be God at all, one may characterize the ontological, essential, or immanent trinity in this way: by the *one substance* of God is properly meant the one God who, as the concrete primal source of all things as well as of our authentic existence, is the one universal, all-inclusive individual who both loves and is loved by self and all others. By the *three persons* of God, on the other hand, we properly understand the abstract distinctions necessarily involved in the individuality of God as this one universal individual—specifically: (1) God's *individuality as such*, as the universal individual who both loves and is loved by self and all others (God the Father); (2) God's *objectivity*, or individuality in respect of being *loved by* Godself and all others (God the Son); and (3) God's subjectivity, or individuality in respect of *loving* all, both Godself and all others (God the Holy Spirit).

So far as the *person* of the Spirit is concerned, then, the Spirit who economically, or from the standpoint of revelation, is the *empowering* primal source of obedient faith working through love is essentially, ontologically, or immanently God as universal *subject* of love—just as the person of the Son who economically is the *entitling* primal source of authenticity is essentially God as universal *object* of love—of God's own love as well as of all creaturely love.

As for the *work* of the Holy Spirit, if what is in question is the Spirit's so-called external work, or work *ad extra*, it neither is nor can be anything other than the external work of the Father and of the Son, also—according to the ancient rule that "the external works of the trinity are undivided [among the three persons]" (*opera trinitatis ad extra indivisa sunt*). The work *ad extra* of the triune God, and hence also of the Holy Spirit is to create and consummate, to emancipate and redeem, and—in the case of human beings and any other beings fallen into sin—also to save. This means, so far as we are concerned, that God works not only to give us existence and to free us from our bondage to decay by embracing our lives within God's own life, but also to save us from sin, by entitling and empowering us once again to entrust our lives solely to God's love and to serve faithfully God's cause alone, notwithstanding our having always already existed in unfaith and idolatry, in distrust and disloyalty.

To be sure, there is also in the theological tradition the doctrine of "trinitarian appropriations," according to which the triune God's external work of creation and emancipation may be "appropriated" to the person of the Father, while the external work of consummation and redemption, insofar as it pertains to sinful creatures as justification and sanctification, may be similarly "appropriated" to the persons of the Son and the Spirit respectively. The effect of this doctrine of so-called appropriations, however, is too often to preserve the insight that the external work of any one of the divine persons is not to be divided from that of the others only by subtly undermining it.

Be this as it may, the result of the Spirit's work in salvation is not different from that of the Father and the Son. Because God is the triune God and is also *our* God, confronting each of us here and now with the gift and demand of love, we both are and ought to be radically free— free both *from* and *for* ourselves and the world within the encompassing security and challenge of God's love. Insofar, then, as I appropriate God's prevenient love by responding in obedient faith and returning love to God's own entitling and empowering presence in *my* life, to that extent my life is both a *liberated* life, freed from the power as well as the guilt of sin, and also a *liberating* life, free for all things, to love and to serve them and thereby to help to set them free.

I trust it will be clear enough by now that, in thus developing the doctrine of the Holy Spirit, I have not at all departed from the procedure I have been concerned to follow in previous discussions. In beginning, as I have in this chapter, with Christian faith and experience, I have still begun, in effect, with Christian witness and its constitutive christological assertion that Jesus is of decisive significance for human existence because he decisively re-presents the meaning of God for us, and so the meaning of ultimate reality for us. I say I have begun with this assertion "in effect" because it is precisely Christian faith and experience that this christological assertion, in one formulation or another, makes explicit. In the present chapter, however, our attention is focused on the necessary implications of this assertion, and thus of the Christian faith and experience that it expresses, otherwise than in the preceding and following discussions. In this case, we have focused our attention neither on creation nor human existence, nor even on the person and work of Jesus Christ or the being and acting of the triune God. Instead, we have focused it on the meaning of God for us as the presence empowering our own existence in obedient faith as well as our existence and all other creaturely existence simply as such. But the connection with the constitutive christological assertion should be clear, for we have Paul's testimony that, if "no one can say 'Jesus is Lord' except by the Holy Spirit," it is also true, conversely, that "no one speaking by the Spirit of God ever says, 'Jesus be cursed'" (1 Cor 12:3).

5.4. LIFE IN THE SPIRIT

It is the liberated and liberating life just referred to, the life of radical freedom grounded in God's prevenient love decisively re-presented through Jesus Christ as attested by the Holy Spirit through the church's witness of faith—it is this kind of life that is life in the Holy Spirit, or, as Paul can also say, life "according to the Spirit" (κατὰ πνεῦμα). As such, it is at once (1) *the mode of existence* of all who respond to God's prevenient love in obedient faith, in trust and loyalty, and in returning love, and (2) *the ever-new act* of existing to which they are called again and again anew in every moment of their existence. In other words, life in, or according to, the Spirit must be described dialectically, or paradoxically, in both indicative and imperative terms, following Paul's lead when he says to the Galatians, "If we live in the Spirit, let us also walk in the Spirit" (Gal 5:25).

I ask the reader to recall the strict parallel here that I pointed out earlier between existence in the Spirit and existence in sin. In both cases, there is the same dialectical, or paradoxical, relationship between (1) *mode* of existence; and (2) ever-new *act* of existing. We *are* sinners, existing in the state or condition of sin, only in and through our own ever-new *act* of sinning, just as our own ever-new act of sinning is the expression of our state or condition, our mode of existence, as sinners. Similarly, we *are* existing in the Spirit, or according to the Spirit, only in and through our own ever-new *act* of obedient faith working through love, just as this ever new act of trust in God's love and loyalty to God's cause itself expresses our new *mode* of existence in the Spirit.

As for the chief defining characteristic of living in the Spirit, as well as of the walking in the Spirit in which it consists, it is, quite simply, love—

in the sense of loyalty to God and hence to all to whom God is loyal, and therefore the acceptance of one's neighbor as oneself and the active service of all creaturely needs in which such acceptance finds expression. It is, in Paul's phrase, "faith working through love" (Gal 5:6)—and, as I like to add, love incarnating itself as justice. Thus, even as the "works of the flesh," according to Paul, are "immorality, impurity, licentiousness, idolatry, sorcery, enmity, strife, jealousy, anger, selfishness, dissension, party spirit, envy, drunkenness, carousing, and the like," so "the fruit of the Spirit" is "love, joy, peace, patience, kindness, goodness, faithfulness, gentleness, self-control" (Gal 5:22–23).

But here we need to emphasize that this life of love and service that is life in, or according to, the Spirit both can and must be lived out in every sphere of our existence in the world and, therefore, through *all* the forms of society and culture, secular as well as religious. It is to be lived out *explicitly* through the forms of religion, but also *implicitly* through all the secular social and cultural forms: morality, politics, science, the arts, and so on. In every sphere, however, the one proof of love, and hence of life in or according to the Spirit, is whether what we think, say, or do edifies or builds up. So, in Paul's words to the Corinthians, "Let all things be done for edification, to build up" (1 Cor 14:26).

As for what it means to live in such a way as a representative minister of the church and, therefore, indirectly, also a professional theologian, it means, above all, to cultivate and to exercise the gift of the Spirit that Paul refers to in 1 Corinthians 12 as "the ability to distinguish between spirits." Certainly, this is not the only, or even the primary, gift of the Holy Spirit—as should be clear enough simply from its reflexive character: unless there is something already present that at least claims to be the work of the Spirit, it would be neither possible nor necessary to test this claim by distinguishing between spirits. But although there are indeed, as Paul says, varieties of gifts, even as there are varieties of service and varieties of working, none is more essential to leading the church or to reflecting critically on the meaning and validity of its witness than the gift of distinguishing between spirits—between what is, indeed, of the Spirit of God and what is of some other spirit, which always means, finally, the evil or demonic spirit that destroys and tears down, instead of creating and building up true human existence and community.

There is an old saying, much beloved by Martin Luther, according to which "one teaches well who distinguishes well." I wholeheartedly accept this teaching, and would add only that it can and should be generalized to cover not only teaching but also the whole work of any leader of the church as well as of any theologian. But, then, the manifestation of the Spirit for which all persons called to leadership of the church especially need to pray is the ability to distinguish between spirits. And if their prayer is serious and more than words, it will be toward the cultivation of just this ability that they will feel obliged to work—and to work continually, in all that they think, say, and do.

6

On the Church

6.0. PRELIMINARY REMARKS

As I shall develop it, this discussion of the church will have to do respectively with what constitutes the church, or with what the church re-presents, and with what the church, in turn, constitutes, or with what re-presents the church. With respect to the first, I shall be raising and answering three main questions: (1) What constitutes the church as the church? (2) What is the distinctive function of the church? (3) What are the obligations of church membership? With respect to the second, I shall speak to the single main question: (4) What are the means by which the church performs its distinctive function? This, then, explains the division of the discussion into its four main sections.

Throughout it, I shall be operating with the same basic concepts-terms I have employed especially in the two preceding discussions of Jesus Christ and the Holy Spirit. I refer to all the concepts-terms related to the key ideas of "authority" and "authorization." I recall the summary statement of my christology in the formulation that Jesus Christ is the event through which God decisively authorizes our authentic existence as an existence of obedient faith in God's prevenient love and, on the basis of this faith, of returning love for God and for all whom God loves. Then, in formulating my doctrine of the Holy Spirit, I argued from the assumption that such authorization, like any other properly so-called, has two distinct but inseparable aspects: it *entitles* us, or gives us the *right*, to such an existence of faith working through love and love incarnating itself in justice; and it *empowers* us, or gives us the *power*, to exist in this way. With this argument in view, I had already proposed in the discussion of God that, although we do not *have to* talk about the trinity, and thus the Holy Spirit, we nonetheless *may and should* talk about the Holy Spirit as God's own presence and power enabling us to exist in obedient faith working through love, even as we may also talk about the Son as the Word, or essential rationale of this same divine presence, that entitles us, or gives us the right, so to exist. In this connection, I made clear that Jesus Christ as the event through which this Word of God is decisively re-presented is the explicit *primal authorizing source* of obedient faith working through love and love incarnating itself in justice, while the normative witness of the apostles is the *primary authority* authorized by this primal source through the Holy Spirit.

But now, in the tradition of the churches of the Reformation in which I stand, to talk about the church—more exactly, the *visible* church—is to talk about the community constituted by just this normative apostolic witness. Thus, according to Paul, God was in Christ reconciling the world to himself and entrusting to us, which is to say, to all of us who are given and called to share in the vocation of the apostles, the ministry and the word of reconciliation (2 Cor 5:18ff.).

The basic ideas I want to develop further, then, are: (1) the idea of the triune God as the *implicit* primal source of authentic existence in faith working through love and love incarnating itself as justice; (2) the idea of Jesus Christ as the *explicit* primal source authorizing such an existence, and, more exactly, *entitling* us so to exist; (3) the idea of the Holy Spirit as the other essential aspect of *empowering* belonging to this primal source both as implicit in our existence as such and as explicit in the normative witness of the apostles to Jesus Christ; and (4) the idea of the visible church as the community having the authority authorized by the explicit primal source, which is to say, the community that is both entitled by Jesus Christ and empowered by the Holy Spirit to exist in this way and thus to be the primary authority authorizing such existence.

It will be noted that these few basic ideas involve two equally basic distinctions: (1) between *primal source of authority* and *primary authority*; and (2) between *implicit* and *explicit* primal source of authority. So far as the first distinction is concerned, suffice it to say that, although every authority is also a source of authority, the converse statement is not and cannot be true, that every source of authority is also an authority in the same sense of the word. Any authority properly so-called derives its authority from some authorizing source that gives it its right and its power. But, then, there neither would nor could be any authority at all unless it derived from a primal authorizing source whose own right and power, being *primal*, are and must be, precisely, not derived. Assuming, then, that, for Christians, as for radical monotheists generally, God is the only *primal* authorizing source, one can never properly speak of God as being *an* authority, as distinct from saying that God *has* authority. If God were *an* authority, even the *highest* authority, there would have to be some other source whence God's authority derived. As for the second distinction, it belongs to the very meaning of "God," in the radically monotheistic way of talking about strictly ultimate reality, that God must be somehow present in anything that is so much as possible and, therefore, must be at least implicitly present in all of our experience and understanding, in all that we think, say, or do. Moreover, on the Christian understanding, the God who is and must be at least implicitly present to every human being as soon and as long as she or he really is such is none other than the triune God—Father, Son, and Holy Spirit—at least implicitly authorizing, i.e., entitling and empowering, an existence in obedient faith and returning love as our only authentic existence. But it is no other or less than this same God who is decisively re-presented through Jesus Christ as explicitly authorizing the same kind of existence as alone authentically human. Therefore, the event of Jesus Christ is nothing other or less than the same authorizing source implicitly present in every human existence, only now become explicit in a decisive way.

6.1. THE CONSTITUTION OF THE CHURCH

With this much by way of a further clarification of certain basic concepts and distinctions, I turn to the first of the three questions I want to raise and answer: What constitutes the church as the church? In addressing it, I find it helpful, and even necessary, also to employ certain traditional distinctions that figure prominently in the ecclesiology developed by Protestant orthodox theology.

Especially important is the fundamental distinction between (1) the church in the strict or proper sense (*ecclesia stricte s. proprie dicta*) and (2) the church in the broad sense (*ecclesia late dicta*). The church strictly or properly spoken of is otherwise called the invisible church (*ecclesia invisibilis*), while the church broadly spoken of is the visible church (*ecclesia visibilis*). Or, again, this same distinction is expressed by distinguishing between (1) the church of the elect or chosen, i.e., the community of the truly faithful and holy (*ecclesia electorum s. coetus vere credentium et*

95

sanctorum); and (2) the church or community of the called (*ecclesia s. coetus vocatorum*). On my view, this distinction, however made, remains an absolutely essential ecclesiological distinction, despite the objections that are not uncommonly made to it. Usually, these objections turn out to rest on the assumption that the purpose of the distinction is to distinguish somehow between an ideal, and therefore true, church, on the one hand, and the actual, and therefore less than true, or even false, church, on the other hand. But this assumption is totally without warrant, so far, at least, as the traditional orthodox distinction is concerned. The ground of *this* distinction is really the necessarily invisible nature of faith working through love, in the strict sense of the words. Whether or to what extent any person so responds to God's call as really and truly to accept it in authentic faith and love is a judgment that God alone is competent to make. For faith and love in the strict sense are matters of the "inner person," or of the "heart," and so only God is competent to judge of their presence or absence. On the other hand, orthodoxy rightly holds that you and I are in principle competent to judge, and therefore have the right as well as the responsibility to judge, as to the boundaries of the visible church. For what constitutes the visible church is itself something visible, namely, the preaching of the pure word of God and the right administration of the sacraments, together with the public profession of the Christian witness of faith in response to them. Thus, according to the Articles of Religion of my own United Methodist Church, for example, "the visible Church of Christ" is said to be "a congregation of faithful [women and] men in which the pure Word of God is preached, and the Sacraments duly administered according to Christ's ordinance, in all those things that of necessity are requisite to the same" (Article XIII).

Working in terms of this same distinction, then, I should say that the essential nature of the church is that it is, in the case of the invisible church, the community of authentic faith working through love in response to the gracious acceptance of God, while, in the case of the visible church, it is the community of valid Christian witness both explicit and implicit. Therefore, what constitutes the invisible church is, in the first place, God's acceptance and the call to each and every human being that God's acceptance at least implies; and, in the second place, women's and men's acceptance of God's acceptance through the obedient faith that works through love incarnating itself as justice. On the other hand, what constitutes the visible church is, in the first place, the decisive re-presentation of God's acceptance through Jesus Christ and the explicit call to faith and love that it issues to all who can receive it; and, in the second place, valid witness to Jesus Christ through the works of faith working through love, both explicitly, through the social and cultural forms of religion, and implicitly, through all of the other so-called secular forms of society and culture.

There are, to be sure, certain differences between this understanding of what constitutes the church and that presupposed by the traditional Protestant orthodox distinction in terms of which I have expressed it. The reader may well have noted one of these differences when I said just now that the visible church is constituted, not by preaching the pure word of God and rightly administering the sacraments, but simply by bearing the Christian witness of faith. By saying this, I mean to reject the classical Protestant view that the visible church is constituted by word and sacraments.

There are two reasons for this rejection. First of all, this classical view betrays a "*religious* bias," in the sense that it understands the church to be constituted solely by the *explicit* witness of faith, rather than, as I maintain, by *both* explicit *and* implicit witness. One consequence of this bias is that the responsibility of Christians in and for the whole of human society and culture has been made to seem at best something inessential or unimportant, at worst something that they can safely ignore or neglect. Although I am far from supposing that the Christian life can be led *solely* in "secular," or "nonreligious" terms, I am profoundly convinced that it must *also* be led in such terms.

But a second reason for rejecting the classical Protestant understanding of the visible church's constitution is that it also betrays what I call a "*clerical* bias," in favor of the representative forms of the explicit witness constitutive of the visible church. Preaching the word and administering the sacraments, together, of course, with hearing the word and receiving the sacraments, are not the only forms, although they are the *representative* forms, of the explicit witness of faith. Again, my point is not to question the great importance of preaching and sacraments and, as I should add, of a representative ministry whose office it is, centrally, to preach the word and administer the sacraments. But what is important, even of great importance, to the church is one thing, what constitutes the church, something else. And, in my view, preaching and sacraments as well as the representative ministry are not constitutive even though they are of great importance. Put differently, they are not constitutive *of* the church, but rather constituted *by* the church, and so *representative* of it. There not only can be, but also obviously has been, a visible Christian church even in the absence of the preaching and the sacraments that the Reformation definitions of the church typically take to be essential to, or constitutive of, it. This is clear not only from the existence of an indisputably Christian community such as the Society of Friends, for instance, but also from the earliest apostolic community itself—about which we know nothing certain to the contrary. On the other hand, there cannot be a visible church at all without the witness of faith that is the obligation of each and every individual Christian as well as of the community thereof.

In sum: I differ from the classical Protestant understanding of the visible church by trying to overcome, at last, both the religious and the clerical biases that, as it seems to me, distort the understanding of the church implied by the apostolic witness.

I also differ at a crucial point from the classical Protestant understanding of the invisible church. On that understanding, membership in the visible church of word and sacrament, although not a *sufficient* condition of membership in the invisible church of the truly faithful and holy, is nonetheless a *necessary* condition of such membership. Therefore, although being a member of the visible church is no guarantee that one also belongs to the invisible church, there can be no question of one's belonging to the second unless one also belongs to the first. In my view, by contrast, the call to membership in the invisible church is by no means simply identical with the call to membership in the visible church. The first call, I believe, is the universal call of God issued at least implicitly to every human being in every moment of her or his existence, and the only condition for accepting *this* call is the acceptance of one's own existence and of all existence as unconditionally accepted—as an existence, therefore, always already freed *from* the burden of the past and freed *for* the responsibility of the future. It is this same call at least implicitly addressed to every woman and man that is then addressed to all who can hear it not only explicitly but decisively through Jesus Christ as attested by the Christian witness of faith. Therefore, although entrance into the visible church neither is nor can be the only entrance to the invisible church, the only invisible church there either is or can be is the community of accepting God's acceptance through obedient faith working through love and love incarnating itself as justice, to which the visible church is the entrance. This means, among other things, that, although I cannot say of the *visible* church, much less of any institutional church, that "outside the church no salvation" (*extra ecclesiam nulla salus*), I do not hesitate to say this of the *invisible* church. For to be saved and to be a member of the invisible community constituted by God's prevenient love through obedient faith working through returning love are one and the same thing. It also means that I can say of the invisible church in relation to the world what Frederick Denison Maurice says of it—namely, "the world contains the elements of which the church is composed. In the church, these elements are penetrated by a uniting, reconciling power. The church is, therefore, human society in its normal state; the world, that same society irregular and abnormal. The world is the church without God; the church is the world restored to its relation with God, taken back by [God] into the state for which [God] created it."[1]

There are two more points I need to make before moving to the next question. The first is to insist on yet a further distinction between the *visible church*, on the one hand, and the *institutional church or churches*, on the other. The visible community traditionally spoken of by Protestant theology and also spoken of in the reformulated doctrine of the church I am outlining here is never to be simply identified with the institutional church or churches, either individually or collectively. The reason for this is shrewdly brought out in the Westminster Confession, when it is said that the visible church "hath been sometimes more, sometimes less, visible" (28:4). In other words, what is meant by the visible church is like what is meant by the Christian witness of faith, which is never given simply as such as one witness, but is always given only in and through all of the many witnesses and kinds of witness, being only more or less adequately expressed in any of them and so simply identifiable with none of them. So, too, with the visible church, which we actually encounter only in and through all the many institutional churches, but which is only more or less visible in each of them and, therefore, cannot be simply identified with any of them, either severally or together. Even if all the institutional churches were to be united into one institutional church, or, at least, one community of institutional churches bound together by universal intercommunion, there would still be an important difference between that

1. Maurice, *Theological Essays*, 276–77.

institutional church or community of institutional churches and the visible church of which I have been speaking.

Significantly, this point once seemed to have been officially conceded, in however guarded a way, even by the Roman Catholic Church. At any rate, according to the teaching of the Dogmatic Constitution on the Church of Vatican Council II, any simple identification of the visible church with the Roman Catholic Church would be incorrect; for "the one Church of Christ which in the symbol of faith is professed as one, holy, catholic, and apostolic ... subsists in the Catholic Church which is governed by the successor of Peter and by the Bishops in his communion, although many elements of sanctification and of truth are found outside of its visible structure" (I, 8). Something like this, in my judgment, is the very most that any Christian has the right to say concerning her or his institutional church. For the church a Christian confesses faith in when she or he says, "I believe ... in the holy catholic church," or, in the words of the Nicene Creed, "I believe ... in one, holy, catholic, and apostolic church," is no institutional church but the visible church—and, through it, of course, also the invisible church of which the visible church is the primary sign.

This brings me to the other point I need to make concerning the essential nature, or constitution, of the Christian church: the visible church, albeit in the nature of the case a particular human community among others, has a strictly universal significance. Having, as it does, the apostolic authority authorized by the primal authorizing source of God through Jesus Christ and the Holy Spirit, it is itself the primary sign or sacrament of the world's redemption and thus of the salvation of all humankind. Here I would appeal to the definition of the church offered by Vatican Council II, according to which the church is "the sacrament of the salvation of the whole world" (*sacramentum salutis totius mundi*).

> [I]n the conciliar text [Karl Rahner interprets], the church is not the society of those who alone are saved, but the sign of the salvation of those who, as far as its historical and social structure are concerned, do not belong to it. By their profession of faith, their worship and life, the human beings in the church form as it were the one expression in which the hidden grace promised and offered to the whole world emerges from the abysses of the human soul into the domain of history and society. What is there expressed may fall on deaf ears and obdurate heart in the individual and may bring judgment instead of salvation. But it is the

sign of grace which brings what it expresses, and not only in cases where it is heard in such a way that the hearer [her- or] himself visibly and historically joins the band of those who announce and testify to this word of God to the world. The church is the sacrament of the salvation of the world even where the world is still not and perhaps never will be the church. It is the tangible, historical manifestation of the grace in which God communicates [Godself] as absolutely present, close, and forgiving, of the grace which is at work everywhere, omits no one, offers God to each and gives to every reality in the world a secret purposeful orientation towards the intrinsic glory of God ... [T]he church is not simply the sign of God's mercy for those who explicitly belong to it. It is the mighty proclamation of the grace which has already been given for the world, and of the victory of this grace in the world.[2]

In the same vein, Juan Luis Segundo argues that, if the church is necessary, this is not because its absence would mean the absence of grace in the world, but because without the church the grace always already given to the world would not be adequately signified. Thus, so far from being a different road from that traveled by all other women and men, which Christians travel thanks to some special privilege granted exclusively to them by God's revelation in Christ, the Christians' road is "the same road" traveled by all, i.e., "the road of self-giving through love." Christians differ from other human beings only in that, through God's decisive revelation in Christ, "they know the mystery of the journey [on which all are embarked]. And what they know, they know in order to make a contribution to the common quest." Theirs is not "a different road," but "a new responsibility."[3] Thus the visible church is the community of those who know, and who have been given to know, in order to bear witness to those who do not know in the same explicit way in which the church does.

This characteristic note of much recent Roman Catholic theology seems to me to be the profoundest yet struck in the contemporary doctrine of the church. For, in the New Testament understanding of the matter, the essential nature of the visible church is to be the particular sign of God's universal saving will, God's will that not only Christians, but also all women and men everywhere should be saved. To be sure, one could—and, in my view, should—say that it is Jesus Christ himself, not the church, who is the *primal* sacrament of God's universal grace, just as he alone is

2. Rahner, *Christian of the Future*, 82–83.

3. Segundo, *Community Called Church*, 32, 24.

the explicit *primal* source authorizing authentic existence. But there is no getting around the fact that, if this primal sacrament is a sacrament for *all* women and men, and therefore is to continue to be present to them as the sacrament it is, this can happen only in and through the visible church as the human community constituted by valid witness to Jesus Christ. It is solely in and through this witness that Jesus Christ himself is concretely present as the explicit primal source authorizing our authentic existence, and thus as the primal sacrament of God's grace. In this sense, or for this reason, the visible church itself, though not the primal sacrament of God's saving will, is rightly said to be its *primary* sacrament—the primary sign established in the world that the ultimate meaning of human existence, as of all existence, is unconditional acceptance by a love for which nothing is merely indifferent because everything is of everlasting worth.

6.2. THE DISTINCTIVE FUNCTION OF THE CHURCH

In turning now to our second question, What is the distinctive function of the church? we should note, first of all, that it asks about the function of the *visible* church; and then, secondly, that the answer to be given to this question has already been given, in effect, by what has just been said about the constitution of the church, and, specifically, of the visible church. If, as I have argued, the visible church, and hence any institutional church in which it becomes more rather than less visible, is constituted to be the primary sign or sacrament of the whole world's salvation, then, clearly, the distinctive function of the visible church can be nothing other than to be just such a sign or sacrament.

Of course, this overlap between our two questions is only to be expected, insofar as to ask about the constitution of something is usually to ask, sooner or later, about its distinctive function, since what it is constituted to be is nothing, finally, other than what it is distinctively to do. In any case, the distinctive function of the visible church is to bear the witness of faith by which it itself is constituted as the visible church. It exists in order to bear this witness to the world—to each and every human being, whose own vocation, at least implicitly given in the very constitution of her or his existence simply as human, is the same vocation to faith working through love, and love incarnating itself as justice, to which she or he is explicitly, indeed, decisively, called through the Christian witness of faith. Otherwise put, the distinctive function of the visible church is to give *explicit* answer to the universal human question—the *existential* question about the ultimate meaning of human life—by mediating the answer given decisively through Jesus Christ. So, as Segundo rightly says, although the road traveled by the visible church is none other than the road traveled by all human beings—"the road of self-giving through love" whose beginning and end is the unconditional acceptance of God's grace—Christians have been given the privilege, which, like all privileges, is also the responsibility, of making this road explicitly known to all the others who, if only implicitly and inadequately, are also traveling it with them. Or, as Rahner puts it, picking up the ancient metaphor of the militant church, the Christian

> . . . will regard [her- or] himself and other professed Christians as only the advance party of those who, on the roads of history, are traveling to God's salvation and eternity. The church for [her or] him is something like the uniformed units in God's array, the point at which the inner character of divinized [human] life is manifested in tangible historical and sociological form or, rather, in which it is most clearly manifested, because, to the enlightened gaze of faith, grace does not entirely lack visible embodiment even outside the church.[4]

Of course, the distinctive function of the visible church to bear valid witness to Jesus Christ could be expressed otherwise than by analogy with the sacraments. For reasons I will presently explain, preaching and sacraments are both representative forms of the one word or witness of faith, preaching being correctly understood only as an audible sacrament, even as sacraments are correctly understood only as "visible word." Moreover, the church is authorized, or, at least, rightly claims authority, to teach religious truth and, therefore, by implication, metaphysical and moral truth as well. For this reason, the church has been, and quite rightly can be, understood by analogy with a school, or with a corps of teachers and learners charged with the responsibility of educating the human race. But the point of this or any such analogy is to express the distinctive function of the church to be the authorized witness of God to the world, the community of those to whom, through God's reconciling of the world to Godself through Christ, has been committed the word and the ministry of reconciliation (2 Cor 5:18ff.).

4. Rahner, *Christian of the Future*, 84.

6.3. THE OBLIGATIONS OF CHURCH MEMBERSHIP

This brings us to our third question: What are the obligations of church membership? I have argued that one becomes a member of the invisible church by accepting God's acceptance through obedient faith working through love, and that one becomes a member of the visible church because, or insofar as, one joins in bearing valid witness, implicitly as well as explicitly, to Jesus as the Christ, as the one through whom God's acceptance is decisively re-presented. If we ask, then, concerning the obligations of those who are members of the visible church, the answer must be that they are all the obligations entailed by the church's one integral function to bear valid witness to Jesus Christ as the decisive revelation of God. This means, specifically, that all who belong, or would belong, to the visible church are obligated not only to make effective use of the church's witness and of all the specific means whereby it carries out this witness, but also, and above all, to join in the valid administration of this witness and of the specific means of bearing it to all others. Simply put, any member of the visible church is obligated both to accept the church's ministry to her- or himself and to share in the church's ministry to the world—both to be ministered unto and to minister, both to be served and to serve. This means, of course, that anyone who belongs to the visible church, or would belong to it, can accept the privileges of membership only by also accepting its responsibilities. And this implies, in turn, that any member of the church must always be concerned, first of all, for the world, for all humankind, for whose sake the church exists, and then, to this end, must also be concerned for the church, for the validity of the church's witness, for its own clarity and transparency, as the primary sign or sacrament of God's universal grace.

Perhaps I should say that here is a point where I sense that my own theological thinking is in process of undergoing a certain change. Like many others of my generation who have sharply reacted against the traditional ecclesiocentrism of the church, I have usually responded to the question about the obligations of church membership by exclusively focusing on, or, at any rate, by stressing, the obligations of any member, or prospective member, of the church to share in the church's ministry to the world. This is, of course, in keeping with the Pauline teaching that has informed this entire discussion, according to which God's act of reconciling the world to Godself through Christ consists precisely in

God's giving unto all of us who are members of the visible church the ministry or word of reconciliation. Still, I have never entirely forgotten that, given the all-encompassing scope of God's love for us, love and service of others can be authentic only where they are, at one and the same time, authentic love and service of oneself—the self that God loves no less, although certainly no more, than all the other selves and creatures likewise embraced within God's love. Then, too, I have not forgotten that the third of the General Rules of John Wesley's United Societies, and so of my own United Methodist Church, stipulates that one is to evidence one's desire for salvation "by attending upon all the ordinances of God," such as "the public worship of God; the ministry of the Word, either read or expounded; the supper of the Lord; family and private prayer; searching the scriptures; fasting or abstinence." Consequently, I have more and more come to realize that it will not do to stress the obligation to minister to others at the expense of the obligation to allow oneself to be ministered unto by others—and thereby by the One of whom they themselves are all the ministers. But just what this realization means, and how thinking out its implications will eventually affect my answer to this third question, are still not as clear to me as I trust they will become.

What is clear, however—clearer now than ever before—is that being a member of the visible church obliges one to share in the one constitutive ministry of the visible church to bear valid witness to the whole world of God's reconciliation to it and of its reconciliation to God through Jesus Christ. But this means, then, on the one hand, that one is ever obligated both to *interpret* and to *reformulate* the witness that the church has already borne so that it will continue to be credible as well as fitting in the new situation in and for which the church now bears responsibility; and, on the other hand, that one is ever obligated to *discipline* and *reform* the witness that the church is yet to bear so that it will also continue to be appropriate to Jesus Christ in the same situation. The trick, of course, is to keep both of these things in mind without neglecting either of them for the sake of the other. But, in doing either, either interpreting and reformulating the witness of the past, or disciplining and reforming the witness of the future, one must also engage in the kind of critical reflection to which I refer by "theology" in the strict and proper sense of the word. By this I mean that one must so appropriate the church's witness, retrospectively and prospectively, as to validate its claims to be both adequate to its content and fitting to its situation.

This is not to say, naturally, that every member of the visible church is obligated to be a representative, or professional, much less an academic, theologian. To say that would be like saying that, because every member of the church is called to share in the church's ministry to the world, she or he is thereby called to be a representative or professional minister. But just as every member of the church *is* called to be a minister by bearing her or his own valid witness to Jesus Christ, so every member of the church is *also* called to be a theologian by participating in the ongoing process of critical reflection by which the validity claims of the various Christian witnesses and kinds of witness continually need to be critically validated.

If we focus, then, on the relatively active side of our obligations as members of the church, we can summarize them by saying that each of us is obligated *to bear a valid Christian witness* and to see to the validity of the witness borne by the institutional church to which we belong; and then, in order to do precisely this, is also obligated *to reflect critically on the validity of our witness* and of the witness of our church in the larger context of all other Christian witnesses and kinds of witness. I presume, therefore, that a parallel formulation could be offered to summarize the relatively passive side of our obligations as members of the church, in that, if the only witness we are obligated to receive is a valid Christian witness, we are also obligated to engage in the same kind of critical theological reflection without which we could fulfill our primary obligation only by accident. But, as I have said, I have not yet thought all this out as carefully as I need to do.

To avoid a possible misunderstanding of what I have been saying, I want to stress a point I have already made a number of times before— namely, that the church's distinctive function to bear a valid Christian witness, and thus to be the primary sign or sacrament of God's salvation of the world, comprises not only explicit, but also implicit, Christian witness. According to the clear teaching of the synoptic tradition, Jesus came not only preaching the imminent reign or rule of God and its gift and demand to human existence, but also healing illnesses and befriending and sharing his table with many who were marginalized or outcasts in his own society, including women and children. To this extent, Jesus' own witness of faith was not only an explicit witness to the now-occurring event of God's grace, in its gift and demand, but also an implicit witness to this grace that took the form of simple human helpfulness to those who were in need because of their natural or historical circumstances. But the tradition is also quite clear that Jesus understood his healings and his solidarity with the despised as themselves precisely implicit *witness* to the gift and demand of God's rule. "If it is by the finger of God that I cast out demons," he says, "then the reign of God has come to you" (Luke 11:20).

In a similar way, I want to say that each member of the visible church is obligated to bear implicit as well as explicit Christian witness, and this in its representative as well as its constitutive forms. Make no mistake about it, there *are* representative forms of the implicit witness of Christian faith as well as of its explicit witness. Alongside sanctuaries in which the pure word of God is to be preached and the sacraments rightly administered, or church school buildings and schools of theology in which the meaning of valid Christian witness is to be communicated through teaching and learning—these being representative forms of the *explicit* witness of the church—there are homes for older persons and orphaned children, shelters for battered women and the homeless, as well as hospitals, colleges, and universities—all of which are representative forms of the *implicit* witness of faith. Since the witness thus borne implicitly also belongs to the sign function of the church, all the obligations pertaining to bearing witness, and thus to critical theological reflection, also, have an application to it as well. The church is not just the representative church, nor is it a merely religious community. It is, as Dietrich Bonhoeffer puts it, "nothing but a section of humanity in which Christ has really taken form . . . What matters in the church is not religion, but the form of Christ, and its taking form amidst a band of [women and] men."[5] Therefore, the obligations of church membership are all the obligations entailed by "the formation of the church in conformity with the form of Christ."[6]

6.4. THE MEANS BY WHICH THE CHURCH PERFORMS ITS FUNCTION

6.4.0. Preliminary Remarks

I begin this final section by recalling two points already made or implied in preceding ones.

5. Bonhoeffer, *Ethics*, 21.
6. Ibid.

The distinctive function of the visible church, constituted as it is by valid Christian witness, is to be the *primary* sign of the prevenient love of God for each and every creature, including even sinful, self-misunderstanding creatures, and, in this sense, to be "the sacrament of the salvation of the whole world." This means that the visible church itself and as such is the primary means of salvation. Just as it is the only primary authority for Christian faith, witness, and theology, so it is also the only primary sacrament or means of salvation, all other sacraments or means of salvation being secondary, because constituted by the visible church and therefore representative of it.

Even so, there is a valid and important distinction to be made between Christian witness as such and certain representative forms of Christian witness. Correspondingly, and on this basis, a distinction is also to be made between the *whole* visible church (*ecclesia synthetica*) and the *representative* visible church (*ecclesia repræsentativa*). We always need to keep in mind, of course, that there are both explicit and implicit kinds of witness, which in a traditional theology like John Wesley's, are distinguished systematically as respectively "works of piety" and "works of mercy." Accordingly, it is necessary to recognize representative forms of implicit witness, or works of mercy, as well as of explicit witness, or works of piety—witness being borne, as I have just said, as much by founding hospitals and establishing universities as by building churches and schools of theology. But be this as it may, my main point is that the fundamental distinction between Christian witness as such and the representative forms of Christian witness, both implicit and explicit, grounds an important distinction between the visible church as a whole and the representative visible church.

This distinction is essential for answering our fourth question about the means by which the visible church performs its distinctive function; for it enables us both to recognize the crucial point already insisted on, that the visible church is constituted as such solely by the witness of the apostles and the valid continuation of their witness by each and every Christian, and also to allow that there are nonetheless certain representative forms of Christian witness, and thus of the visible church, which, although they are in no way constitutive of the church but constituted by it, are nonetheless genuine "means of salvation" (*media salutis*).

Chief among such representative forms, I should say—although they are by no means the only such forms—are just those singled out in the classic Protestant definitions of the visible church as constitutive of it—namely, preaching the true word of God and rightly administering the sacraments, specifically, the two sacraments of baptism and the Lord's Supper. To these, then, I should add, as yet a third representative form of witness, the ministerial office, in the sense of the special, or representative, ministry of the church. Even though none of these three forms is what has often been called a "constitutive factor" of the visible church, each of them is a representative form of Christian witness, and thus *is* constitutive of the *representative* church—specifically, of the representative form of the *explicit* witness of faith that is constitutive of the visible church as such.

In focusing, as I shall now do, solely on these three representative forms, I emphasize, once again, that I in no way mean that they are the *only* representative forms of Christian witness. Depending on the analytic scheme one might choose to employ, any number of other representative forms could and should be identified and discussed. Nor, as I have tried to make clear, should anyone suppose that the representative forms of the church's witness, and thus of the visible church itself, are exhausted by the representative forms of its *explicit* witness. Nevertheless, however many representative forms one may be led to recognize, the same rule holds good of them as of the three to which I shall confine my subsequent remarks. They are not *constitutive of* the visible church but *constituted by* it, insofar as they are, by their very nature, representative forms of bearing the one witness of faith—the one ministry and word of reconciliation (2 Cor 5:18–19)—that alone is constitutive of, or essential to, the very being of the visible church as such.

In what follows, I wish, first, to speak generally about preaching the word and administering the sacraments; second, to elaborate somewhat on my understanding of the sacrament of baptism; and third, to make a few concluding remarks about the ministerial office. This selection of topics is arbitrary so far as the subject matter itself is concerned and is dictated primarily by the limits of this discussion and by my judgment as to what I can say most helpfully to give at least some idea of the lines along which I would develop the more adequate treatment of the means of salvation that present limitations make impossible.

6.4.1. Preaching the Word and Administering the Sacraments

First, then, a brief comment about preaching the word and administering the sacraments as different, but closely related forms of representing the Christian witness of faith. I want to speak about word and sacraments together because, in my judgment, both are forms of the one Christian kerygma or proclamation, and neither can be so understood as to avoid certain familiar misunderstandings except by being understood in close relation to the other.

Characteristic of Protestant theology since its inception is an understanding of preaching and administering the sacraments as both forms of the one word of God—the kerygma or proclamation through which the eternal word of God's grace originally and implicitly presented to every human existence is explicitly and decisively re-presented by means of particular human words and deeds. Thus Protestant theologians have typically and gratefully appropriated the well-known definition of sacrament by Augustine as "visible word" (*verbum visibile*). This seems to me entirely justified; for on the understanding of grace as God's personal acceptance of all humankind, notwithstanding their sin, which makes possible and requires the personal acceptance of God's acceptance through obedient faith, the only appropriate medium of grace is and must be precisely *word*, in the sense of an explicit intelligible meaning that has to be grasped and laid hold of through the free human response of understanding and, more exactly, self-understanding. The sacraments, therefore, are rightly understood only when they are understood as "*visible* word," as an explicit meaning in the form of a deed or gesture that can be seen as well as heard, but that is a means of salvation if, and only if, it is understood.

At the same time, I should myself want to maintain that preaching the word is itself rightly understood only as "*audible* sacrament" (*sacramentum audibile*), i.e., a deed or gesture that can be heard as well as seen, but whose meaning can be apprehended only as addressed precisely to the understanding—to our self-understanding, or existential understanding of ourselves in relation to others and to God. If sacraments that are not understood as visible word are apt to be misunderstood as magical rites that are somehow effective in us even though they by-pass our own understanding and moral freedom, sermons that are not understood as audible sacraments are almost certain to be misunderstood merely as teaching rather than as proclamation—as words *about* God, rather than as word *of* God.

One concrete implication of this understanding of preaching and sacraments is that the ideal form of the Christian service of worship through which the explicit witness of faith is most fittingly represented is celebration of the Lord's Supper accompanied by a sermon or homily— or vice versa, a sermon or homily accompanied by celebration of the Lord's Supper. The sacramental context of the sermon protects it from being misunderstood as a mere lecture, while the homiletical context of the sacrament keeps it from being misunderstood as an action that is effective somehow magically, independently of the individual's own self-understanding and free decision of faith.

Please do not misunderstand my point here. I in no way intend to undervalue the teaching function of the church and its ministry. Explicit Christian witness, in my understanding, always involves not just one main form but two: not only Christian kerygma or proclamation, whose representative forms are preaching the word and administering the sacraments, but also Christian teaching or instruction. But whereas the witness of proclamation is direct, the witness of teaching is always only indirect. Thus, for example, it is one thing to proclaim, in Paul's words in 2 Corinthians 5:20, "Be reconciled to God"; it is something else to teach, as Paul himself also does in the immediate context of these words, by explaining what reconciliation is and how God has enacted it through Christ, so as to entrust the ministry and the word of reconciliation to us, which is to say, to the whole visible church.

I would add two further comments on preaching the word and administering the sacraments in general.

First, it is of the greatest importance to distinguish clearly and sharply between the *validity* of word and sacraments, on the one hand, and their *effectiveness*, on the other. From the time of the Donatist controversy of the fourth and fifth centuries CE on, the church catholic has maintained, as I believe rightly, that the personal unworthiness of a minister does not affect the validity of the sacraments that she or he administers, since, as Augustine insisted, their true minister is Jesus Christ. Whether or not a sacrament is valid—and I should say the same thing, *mutatis mutandis*, about the audible sacrament of preaching—in no way depends upon the faithfulness of the minister administering it, but solely upon whether or not the sacrament rightly represents Jesus Christ. Pointedly put, it depends on the quality of the minister's Christian and theological education, not on her or his authenticity or on the quality of her or his personal piety or spirituality.

But more than that, there is an important truth in the Roman Catholic doctrine of "the work worked (or performed)" (*opus operatum*) that Protestants have sometimes overlooked—namely, that the validity of the sacrament is also completely independent of the faith of the person receiving it. Again, what makes a sacrament valid is not that it is received by faith, but that it in fact re-presents Jesus Christ, however it may then be received. On the other hand, there is also a precious truth in the Reformation principle, "no sacrament without faith" (*nullum sacramentum sine fide*)—namely, that the effectiveness of a sacrament, as distinct from its validity, *does* depend on the faith of its recipient, even though it in no way depends on the faith of the person administering it. No sacrament is or can be effective, in the sense of achieving the end of a person's salvation, without the obedient faith of that person—not because the gift of God's grace is in some way conditional on our faith, but because salvation, though *by* grace alone, is never without our own faith, *through* which alone we can accept God's unconditional acceptance of us.

I am in no way suggesting by these comments that no serious differences remain between Roman Catholic and Protestant understandings of the means of salvation. But I do want to suggest that at least some of the historic differences clearly seem to be due to overlooking the distinction between the validity of a sacrament, on the one hand, and its effectiveness, on the other.

Incidentally, this distinction has sometimes been made by distinguishing between the "operational potential" (*potentia operandi*) of a means of salvation and its "actual operation" (*operatio actualis*), understanding by the first, the power of a means to produce the desired effect or result, and thus its validity, and by the second, its actualizing this power by actually producing the effect or result desired, and so its effectiveness.

My second comment has to do with the so-called real presence of Jesus Christ in both word and sacraments. This matter is usually discussed in connection with the Lord's Supper. But for reasons that should now be clear, the question of the "real presence" of Christ is also relevant to baptism and preaching, not to mention any other representative form of the explicit witness of faith. The pertinent point is simply that Jesus Christ is really present in preaching and sacraments in the same way in which any person is really present in the words and deeds of direct address that re-present her or his meaning for us. Insofar, then, as preaching and sacraments are representative forms of the direct witness of faith, Jesus Christ himself is really present—namely, *re*-present, present *again*, a *second* time—in them, even as he himself, in turn, is the *decisive* re-presentation of God's own gift and demand of saving grace. The power of the word precisely as direct address is always to re-present him in this way. So wherever the word that Jesus Christ himself is, is itself re-presented—as it clearly is or should be, first of all, in the visible church as such and then, secondly, in both its preaching and its administering the sacraments—he is not merely talked about, as he is in Christian teaching, but is himself really and personally present, as is the saving grace of God of which he is the decisive re-presentation.

6.4.2. *The Sacrament of Baptism*

The essential point to be made about the sacrament of baptism in particular is that it is the means whereby the individual person is decisively called by God through Jesus Christ into the community of faith and witness— or, in other words, into the church in its invisible and visible aspects respectively. Properly understood, baptism is the visible re-presentation through symbolic action of the gracious acceptance of God whereby we are freed *from* our past and freed *for* our future. The water, of course—or, really, the act of being symbolically cleansed by the water—signifies this liberating action of God's grace; and the invocation of the name of Jesus Christ or of the triune God proclaims the primal source of this action and thus also the primal source authorizing the person being baptized to exist henceforth in and for the freedom of faith working through love.

As in the case of the other sacrament of the Lord's Supper, the effectiveness of baptism as a means of salvation presupposes the individual's own decision of faith. In other words, the general principle asserted by the Reformers against their Roman Catholic opponents' *opus operatum* also holds good here: *nullum sacramentum sine fide*—no sacrament without faith. However valid baptism may be, it can be effective if, and only if, the grace it explicitly re-presents is accepted through the personal faith of the person being baptized.

This principle does not mean, however, that the visible witness to God's gracious action through baptism takes place only *because* of the baptized person's faith. On the contrary, the act of baptism is performed solely *because* of God's gracious action, the faith of the person baptized being in no way a cause or condition of the witness borne by the sacrament, any more than it is a cause or condition of God's gracious action. Indeed, we must go still further and say that not even baptism itself, in the sense of the representative form of witnessing to God's action, is in any way a cause or condition of God's action. Baptism does not *constitute* God's gracious action toward a person, but rather *re-presents* it—to her or him as a unique individual as well as to the church and the world.

Here I should like to acknowledge the theological work of the great Anglican preacher of the nineteenth century, F. W. Robertson, who seems to me to provide the only perspective from which a proper view of baptism can be had. Like some of his contemporaries, such as F. D. Maurice and Charles Kingsley, Robertson particularly struggled to understand the language of the Anglican Catechism, according to which the answer to be given to the question about baptism is that it is the event "wherein I was made a member of Christ, the child of God, and an inheritor of the kingdom of heaven." Believing, as he put it, that "baptism could not make me a child of God unless I were one by reason of my humanity already," he sought to identify uses of the verb "to make" that were supportive of his belief. In this connection, he drew several analogies, among them the following:

> The Catechism . . . says: In baptism. . . I was *made* a child of God. Yes; coronation makes a sovereign; but, paradoxical as it may seem, it can only *make* one a sovereign who is a sovereign already. Crown a pretender, that coronation will not make a king. Coronation is the authoritative act of the nation *declaring* a fact which was fact before. And ever after, coronation is the event to which all dates back—and the crown is the expression used for all royal acts. Similarly with baptism. Baptism makes a child of God in the sense in which coronation makes a king. And baptism naturally stands in Scripture for the title of regeneration and the moment of it. Only what coronation is in an earthly way, an authoritative manifestation of an invisible earthly truth, baptism is in a heavenly way: God's authoritative declaration in material form of a spiritual reality. In other words, no bare sign, but a Divine Sacrament.[7]

---

7. Robertson, *Sermons by F. W. Robertson* (second series, 1898 ed.); cited by Vidler, *Theology of F. D. Maurice*, 56–57.

Baptism is an authoritative symbol of an eternal fact; a truth of eternity realised in time, and brought down to the limits of "then and there": then and there made God's child. But it is only the re-alisation of a fact true before baptism, and without baptism: the personal realisation of a fact which belongs to all humanity, and was revealed by Christ; in other words, [baptism] is redemption applied.[8]

These passages seem to me to make beautifully clear the radically unconditional and prevenient character of God's action, which it is pre-cisely the function of baptism to body forth in a visible and symbolically powerful way. God does not love because the church baptizes; the church baptizes because God loves. But equally important, this is the *only* reason the church baptizes, and not also because the person baptized first has faith or makes a public profession of faith. It was no part of the Reformers' intention in insisting on the inseparable connection of faith and sacra-ment to question *this* point. On the contrary, the whole import of their watchword, "grace alone" (*sola gratia*), was precisely to rule out any such distortion of baptism, as they were compelled to regard it.

On the other hand, the Reformers made quite clear that baptism can be an effective means of salvation to the individual baptized if, and only if, she or he, *through faith*, personally appropriates the grace of which it is the visible witness. And this, of course, is where a certain difficulty arises. If baptism can be an effective sacramental action, a real witness to grace actually received as such, only on condition of the faith of the person baptized, then what are we to make of the historical practice of baptizing infants?

I hardly have to say that this remains a question for us today—espe-cially if we happen to live in a society and culture significantly influenced by the Baptist tradition of baptizing only adults who have already publicly professed their faith prior to baptism. Unfortunately, I do not have space for an adequate discussion of this question. Nor can I say very much about the ways in which the historic Protestant churches that have continued the practice of infant baptism have nonetheless sought to defend it. I must be content simply with laying down some principles that seem important to me if any adequate answer to the question is to be had.

First, one should keep in mind what has already been said—namely, that the whole point of baptism, as indeed of preaching and of the Lord's

8. Brooke, ed., *Life and Letters of Frederick W. Robertson, M.A.*, vol. 2, 62.

Supper, is to witness to the radical prevenience of God's grace, i.e., the pure, unbounded nature of God's love and the unconditional character of God's acceptance. But what more powerful witness to just this truth can be imagined than the baptism of an infant, who quite obviously has nothing to offer as a condition or claim wherewith to secure God's favor? It is my judgment that the most important reason for continuing the practice of infant baptism is to be found precisely here.

Second, however, it is important to recognize that this defense of infant *baptism* in no way prejudices the very different question of infant *confirmation*. So far as I can see, the chief objections usually brought against infant baptism are really telling only against infant confirmation, i.e., the, to my mind, very un-Protestant idea that the person baptized can somehow enter life in the community of faith and witness opened up to her or him through baptism without her or his own individual faith and witness. For my own part, this idea is indeed mistaken and cannot possibly be justified. But what I do not see is why this constitutes any reason for objecting to infant *baptism*.

At the same time, I must say, third, that the practice of infant baptism can be justified only where there is also something like the rite of confirmation, i.e., a rite in which the baptized infant now come of age is publicly confirmed in her or his baptism and also confirms for her- or himself the faith witnessed by her or his baptism. I do not mean by this, of course, that the grace re-presented to one in one's baptism can be effective only where there is such a public witness. On the contrary, the only condition necessary for receiving grace, whether as re-presented in baptism or otherwise, is faith; and as I have tried to emphasize, such faith is not simply identical with a public profession of Christian faith such as confirmation properly requires. On the other hand, faith itself, by its very nature, compels or makes imperative just such a public confession as well as an outward witness through the whole of one's life, secular as well as religious. Precisely *because* one comes to faith, one finds oneself unavoidably driven to witness to one's faith in the outward and visible forms of word and deed. I contend, therefore, that the practice of infant baptism, which seems to me entirely justified, can in no way exclude, but, in fact, necessarily requires, something in the way of confirmation. Baptism may very well incorporate the infant into the visible church in the sense that she or he is thereby decisively called, and so ordained, to the life of witness that is the only constitutive ministry of the visible church. But she or he becomes fully a member of the visible church only as and when she or he publicly accepts for her- or himself the responsibility of actively participating in this ministry.

I may add that the age for confirmation obviously should be sufficient to make the assumption of such responsibilities possible and meaningful. Just as no one of us enters upon her or his majority as a citizen of the state until she or he is old enough to assume the responsibilities of citizenship, so no one ought to be confirmed in the church who is not old enough to enter on the responsibilities of membership in it.

6.4.3. *The Ministerial Office*

Finally, I have a few comments on the representative ministry. In my view, there are and can be only two universal ecclesial offices—understanding by "office" in this context binding the functions of ministry to certain individual persons specially called to exercise them.

There is, first, the unique and nontransferable office of the apostles, by whom I mean the immediate witnesses to Jesus as the Christ, through whose witness of faith everyone else who ever becomes a Christian can alone become such. And there is, second, the common or shared office of every other Christian, who is called as such to be a mediate witness to Jesus as the Christ by witnessing through and with the immediate witness of the apostles. To this common office one is explicitly called or ordained by one's baptism as a Christian, and one enters upon the exercise of its functions by publicly joining in the apostolic witness constitutive of the visible church, which entrance is marked symbolically by one's confirmation or something like it. As Luther puts it, "[W]e are all consecrated priests through baptism ... [W]hoever comes out of the water of baptism can boast that [she or] he is already consecrated priest, bishop, and pope, although, of course, it is not seemly that just anybody should exercise the office."[9]

These two offices alone, I believe, are constitutive of the visible church. Therefore, any other ministerial office can only be a nonconstitutive or representative office, binding certain functions of ministry to individual Christians who are specially called by God, secretly and providentially, and then explicitly confirmed in their divine calling by an official, ecclesial call to perform these functions representatively in and for the church.

9. Atkinson, ed., *Luther's Works*, vol 44: *Christian in Society I,* 127, 129.

Although I believe, just as Luther did, that no one has the right to enter upon such a representative ministerial office unless she or he has also been explicitly confirmed in her or his calling by the official call of the visible church, I emphatically dispute the right of any institutional church to establish conditions for issuing such an official call other than those that are strictly necessary to validly exercising the functions of the office. This means, among other things, that I repudiate the historical tradition of making either the male gender or the heterosexual orientation of a Christian a necessary condition of receiving an official, ecclesial call to the representative ministry of the church.

Beyond any question, such a representative ministerial office ordinarily furthers the constitutive ministry of the visible church. And it is entirely fitting that the church's ministry and word of reconciliation should be committed in a special way to those who are called to this office by entrusting to them the other representative functions of preaching the word and administering the sacraments. This is not to say, however, either that these are the only functions of the ministerial office or that they or any of its other functions ought under no circumstances to be performed by anyone other than a representative minister. To this office also belongs the other essential function of Christian teaching or instruction as well as the functions of pastoral care and administration of the life and work of the church. In short, the representative minister is called to lead in all of the forms of bearing Christian witness that belong to the visible church, implicit as well as explicit. Even so, the chief functions of the representative ministry are precisely the explicitly religious functions of Christian proclamation and teaching, and thus of preaching the word and administering the sacraments—not because the church would not be the church without these functions, but because, given the history through which it has passed as well as the future now awaiting it, these functions are of utmost importance to its ministry as the church, just as is the representative ministry to which these functions are ordinarily bound.

More than this, however, I see no reason to say, although I myself recognize in the special ministry of the historic episcopate a special form of the ministerial office that also has much to commend it, considering both the past of the church and its likely future. The critical point is only that episcopacy as such is no more constitutive of the representative church and its ministry than the representative church, in turn, is constitutive of the visible church itself. The church in its visible aspect is constituted solely by the apostolic witness of faith and by the constant renewal of that witness by all baptized Christians, witnessing through and with the apostles to the sole Lordship of Jesus Christ, in the power of the Holy Spirit, to the glory of God the Father. Any other ministry, accordingly, is simply a delimitation of this general Christian ministry, this "priesthood of *all* believers," to certain persons who are specially called to its work and have the special gifts and graces required to represent the church in its one indispensable function of bearing valid Christian witness—or, once again in Paul's terms, of actualizing the ministry and word of reconciliation entrusted to the whole visible church, and so to each and every Christian.

Consequently, the *episcopos*, as, at most, a minister of the ministers of Jesus Christ, is, least of all, constitutive of the visible church of which she or he as bishop is always only the servant. In the words of John Oman:

> The valid distinction was drawn years ago—"And whosoever would be first among you shall be servant of all." The only good work is service, the only power worth striving after is power to serve, and to be a bishop, an overseer, a ruler, rightly understood, is to be first in humility, in readiness to help, in labour, in danger, and, if need be, in indignity ... [To be a bishop is] to be the Church's representative, to utter her thought, and, if need be, to bear her reproach.[10]

10. Oman, *Vision and Authority*, 282–83.

7

On Salvation

7.0. PRELIMINARY REMARKS

THE TWO NECESSARY PRESUPPOSITIONS of the Christian doctrine of salvation are: (1) the universal fact of sin; and (2) the universal fact of the grace of the triune God, decisively re-presented through Jesus Christ as attested implicitly by the Holy Spirit and thence explicitly by the witness of the visible church and its means of salvation.

I can only hope that, by now, the second of these presuppositions will have been clarified as adequately as I am able to clarify it by what I have already had to say about Jesus Christ and the Holy Spirit, the church and the means of salvation. But I will allow myself one further clarifying statement concerning it—namely, that the grace of the triune God, which is decisively re-presented through Jesus Christ as attested by the Holy Spirit and the church, is just as much a universal fact as is the sin from which it is the salvation. In Paul's words in Romans, "all have sinned and fall short of the glory of God" (Rom 3:23). "But where sin increased, grace abounded all the more, so that, as sin reigned in death, grace also might reign through righteousness to eternal life through Jesus Christ our Lord" (Rom 5:20–21).

I cannot explain the Christian understanding of salvation, however, without recalling the main points of what I have already had to say about its other necessary presupposition—namely, sin, and, more exactly, the universal fact thereof. Hence the first section of the discussion—

7.1. THE SIN FROM WHICH WE ARE SAVED

Sin, I have argued, is a properly moral concept only in the broad sense that refers to anything involving distinctively moral freedom at either the categorial level of life-praxis or—as is true of sin—the transcendental level of self-understanding. Thus sin has to do, in the first instance, with who we *are* or how we *exist*, i.e., how we understand ourselves in relation to self, others, and the strictly ultimate whole of reality called "God," as distinct from how we otherwise *act* and what we *do* in leading our lives. As such, sin is properly understood as the negative counterpart to, because it is the lack or privation of, righteousness, in the sense of the right relation to ourselves, others, and God. Therefore, at its root, sin is, negatively defined, *unfaith*, i.e., distrust in and disloyalty to God as the sole primal source and the sole final end of all things; and, positively defined, sin is *idolatry*, i.e., trust in and loyalty to something or someone else besides God as in some way also necessary to our being and meaning as persons.

"Sin" in this sense is subject to three distinctions or qualifications, which allow us to speak of:

(1) *Original* sin, which is sin as a human state or condition, a *mode* of self-understanding or existence—specifically, the *inauthentic* mode of existence that, at its root, is unfaith and idolatry. Thus "original *sin*" is one of our two original human possibilities "before God" (*coram Deo*), the other such possibility being "original *righteousness*," which is the *authentic* mode, state or condition, of existing humanly, the root of which is obedient *faith*, i.e., trust in God and loyalty to God alone.

(2) *Actual* sin, which is sin as a human *act*, as distinct from a state or condition; specifically, it is the act whereby we misunderstand ourselves before God and thus exist in unfaith and idolatry, i.e., distrust in and disloyalty to God, instead of existing in obedient faith, i.e., trust in and loyalty to God alone. Here, again, I would underscore that there is a dialectical or paradoxical relationship between sin as a state, condition, or *mode* of existence, i.e., original sin, and sin as an *act*, i.e., actual sin. Because or insofar as one *exists* inauthentically, in the misunderstanding of oneself and the world before God that seeks the ultimate meaning of one's life in something besides God alone, one also *acts* inauthentically in all that one thinks, says, and does—just as, to consider the relationship the other way around, one *exists* inauthentically only because or insofar as one continues to *act* inauthentically. If one *is* a sinner, one *acts* sinfully; but only if one *acts* sinfully *is* one a sinner.

(3) *Actual sins*, which are the thoughts, words, and deeds that both express sin, original and actual, and misrepresent it to others as their authentic possibility, too, thereby tempting them to sin. Because sin, properly understood, is a moral concept at the transcendental level of moral

freedom, one's thoughts, words, and deeds at the categorial level may be actual sins "before God" even if they are judged to be morally right, either relatively or absolutely, "before human beings or before the world" (*coram hominibus s. coram mundo*). By being morally right *relatively*, I mean morally right given the moral norms conventional to some society or culture relevant for judging the acts in question, whereas by being morally right *absolutely*, I mean morally right given the *trans*social, *trans*cultural commandments of God, grounded in God's will as the Creator, and thus also in the created natures of human beings and of creatures generally. As such, these commandments are the primal source of the moral authority of all conventional social or cultural moral norms, insofar as they are, in fact, morally authorized. Even thoughts, words, and deeds that are morally right, not merely relatively, but absolutely, can at the same time be sinful—namely, because or insofar as they are done out of sin as the faithless, idolatrous, prideful, and self-loving desire to secure the ultimate meaning of one's life, instead of out of obedient trust in God's love alone and loyalty to its cause that all things shall be and become themselves. The importance of this point, given the common identification of sin as simply moral transgression at the categorial level, is hard to exaggerate.

I may also note that, given these distinctions, the further, and often useful, distinction may also be made between sin in the *strict* sense and sin in the *broad* sense, the first referring to original-actual sin, the second, to original-actual sin *together with the actual sins expressing it and re-presenting it to others*. I remark, parenthetically, that a parallel distinction may also be made, *mutatis mutandis*, between faith in the strict sense of obedient trust in, and loyalty to, God alone, and faith in the broad sense that includes the "good works," or "fruit," through which faith working through love is both expressed and re-presented.

So understood, sin is a universal fact, not a modal necessity. By this I mean, as I explained earlier, that the human condition is, as a matter of fact and of freedom, the human predicament, which is to be described, accordingly, by the statistical generalization that (1) a human being is continually inclined thus to misunderstand her- or himself before God; and (2) a human being is born into a humanity for which this statistical generalization already holds good and that, therefore, in its thoughts, words, and deeds, and their complex institutionalization in societies and cultures is already a fallen, self-corrupted humanity.

7.2. SALVATION FROM SIN BY GRACE ALONE THROUGH FAITH ALONE

According to the understanding of Christian faith, it is from this universal fact of sin that we are saved—namely, by the no less universal fact of God's saving grace, which is originally presented to each of us implicitly in every moment of our existence and which is then explicitly re-presented in a decisive way through Jesus Christ. Thus, by "salvation" is properly meant, first of all and fundamentally, the redemptive activity of God whereby the whole of humankind, and thus each and every human being, notwithstanding the universal fact of sin, is accepted into God's own everlasting life—the theological term for this divine activity being "grace." And then, secondly, and in absolute dependence on God's grace, salvation is the activity of a woman or a man through which she or he accepts God's acceptance—the theological term for this human activity being "faith" and, more exactly, "faith working through love," a love that, as I like to say, incarnates itself as justice. Although it is by God's grace alone that we either are or can be saved from both the guilt of sin and its power, not even God's grace can save us, as the uniquely human, understanding and therefore morally free and responsible creatures we are, except through our own self-understanding, through our own free and responsible *re*-action to God's action. Thus even the great Augustine, known down through the Christian centuries as "doctor of grace" (*doctor gratiæ*), rightly holds that the God "who made us without ourselves will not save us without ourselves." So, also, according to the teaching of the Augsburg Confession (Art. 4), we are justified "freely . . . *because of* Christ *through* faith" (*gratis . . . propter Christum per fidem*). Lying behind such formulations, of course, is the Pauline teaching of Ephesians 2:8, that "by grace you have been saved through faith."

7.3. ISSUES IN DEVELOPING THE DOCTRINE OF SALVATION

In this last section, I will briefly discuss seven issues that one must somehow deal with in further developing the doctrine of salvation.

7.3.1. The Nature of Grace

According to a well-known saying of the Reformer, Philip Melanchthon, "grace is not medicine but favor." The counterposition that Melanchthon is arguing against here is the doctrine common in traditional Christian teaching and theology going back at least as far as the early second century CE to Ignatius of Antioch, who speaks of the Lord's Supper as "the medicine of immortality."[1] To the contrary, Melanchthon insists—and in this he is simply following Luther—grace is to be understood only in strictly relational terms as God's "favor" toward us. We today may well prefer to say, instead of "God's favor," "God's acceptance," even as we may choose to speak of our own faith, with Paul Tillich, as our "acceptance of God's acceptance."[2] But, however we translate the term "grace," we need to emphasize that it is the very nature of grace that it should have an "effective," not merely an "imputative," power. In John Wesley's terms, grace received through faith involves not only "*relative* change," or the change in relation whereby God imputes righteousness to us, but also "*real* change," the change whereby our lives are transformed in that we ourselves actually become righteous.

7.3.2. Grace and Freedom

Each of us is saved, if we are, by grace alone and yet not without ourselves—our own free response of faith. In this sense, the proper formula is "by grace alone but not without ourselves" (*sola gratia non sine homine*). Consequently, neither "monergism," according to which salvation is "by grace alone without ourselves" (*sola gratia sine homine*), nor "synergism, " whose formula is "by both grace and ourselves" (*et gratia et homine*), is an adequate theological position, although they remain, along with so-called Pelagianism, the only positions logically open to us as long as grace is understood (or, as I believe, *mis*understood) in nonrelational, instead of relational, terms.

It may be helpful to say just a word here about the so-called exclusive particle, "alone" (*sola*), which the Reformers use to bring out what they understand to be the New Testament teaching concerning salvation. The point of the particle in all of their uses of it is not to rule out all other factors as also being somehow relevant or playing a role in the matter or process in question; its point, rather, is to rule out such other factors as being *primally* or *primarily* relevant or playing any *primal* or *primary* role. Thus, for example, their talk of "scripture alone" (*sola scriptura*) is not at

1. Ignatius *Letter to the Ephesians* 20.
2. Tillich, *Shaking of the Foundations*, 153–63.

all intended to rule out tradition as being relevant or playing some role as a source or a norm of Christian witness; it is intended, rather, to rule out tradition's being *primarily* relevant as a source or a norm, as scripture, in their view, alone can be, or as playing the kind of *primary* role that scripture alone properly plays. So, also, then, with "Christ alone" (*solus Christus*), which is not in the least intended to rule out the church or its means of salvation as also being relevant or playing a role in salvation, but is intended only to deny to them the *primal* relevance or *primal* role that Christ alone has or plays. And so with all of the other uses of the exclusive particle, including, not least, its use in the watchword, "grace alone" (*sola gratia*), which is in no way intended to rule out "faith," but functions solely to deny to faith the same *primal* relevance or role that can be properly claimed only for grace, as well as its use in "faith alone" (*sola fide*), which in no way denies the importance of "good works," but denies only that they have the *primal* importance that belongs only to faith.

7.3.3. Predestination

There is, in my view, a single, not a double, predestination, in that each and every human being is always already accepted by God's grace, and hence called to salvation, while no human being is rejected by God who does not freely and responsibly reject God's acceptance. The reason for this is that the traditional distinction between God's *calling* women and men and God's *choosing* them is rightly understood as a function of their own choosing, without which God's choosing is not and cannot be effective in their individual cases. We are chosen (or not chosen) *by* God only *through* our own choosing (or not choosing).

Still and all, there is, I believe, a legitimate theological motive in traditional doctrines of double predestination. For although God wills only the salvation of each woman and man, and acts solely to this end, God also wills to suffer with any of them in their damnation insofar as they in their freedom reject God's acceptance. In this sense, or to this extent, damnation or reprobation, as much as salvation or election, falls *within* God's all-loving purpose, not outside it.

7.3.4. Universal Salvation vs. Double Destination

Because the fact of God's grace is universal, there is a universal call to salvation issued to each and every human being implicitly in every moment of her or his existence. But a universal *call* to salvation is one thing, universal *salvation itself*, something else. Because the second depends, as we have seen, not only on God's acceptance of all women and men by grace, but also on every one of them individually freely accepting God's acceptance through obedient faith, Christian witness and theology can no more affirm the *actuality* of universal salvation than they can deny its *possibility*, as is done, in fact, by the counterposition of double destination, with its assertion of heaven and hell, eternal salvation and eternal damnation.

7.3.5. Justification and Sanctification

The heart and center of salvation are justification and sanctification, which, though distinct, are inseparably connected. This they are because grace is the only ground, and faith the only condition, of both alike. As justification, our acceptance of God's acceptance of us is, in John Wesley's terms, "*relative* change," forgiveness of the past, freedom from the *guilt* of sin; as sanctification, it is "*real* change," openness for the future, freedom from the *power* of sin. I should add in passing that, on this issue and the one following, as well as on the doctrine of salvation generally, I continue to find Wesley's witness and theology indefinitely more adequate than any other known to me.

7.3.6. Faith and Good Works

Although we are saved through "faith alone" (*sola fide*), we are not saved through "a lonely faith" (*solitaria fide*), a faith unaccompanied by the good works that are, in Paul's term, its "fruit." On the contrary, "faith is never alone" (*fides nunquam solitaria*), because good works are as necessary to faith working through love as actual sins are to original-actual sin. Faith inevitably finds expression in the witness of faith, either implicit or explicit (or in Wesley's terms, either "works of mercy" or "works of piety"), provided only that there is "time and opportunity" to bear it. In this sense, good works are necessary to salvation—not because we are *not* saved through faith alone but precisely because we *are*.

7.3.7. Salvation and Society

Because the sphere of human possibility and responsibility defined by God's grace includes the whole of human existence—the "outer person" as well as the "inner person"—salvation necessarily includes the whole of our life in society as well as our life as individuals, in that it is salvation from sins as well as from sin, and for good works, or love incarnating itself as justice, as well as for faith working through love. But this has a clear implication for us today that Christians have not always understood it to have—many of them even now. Because of our distinctively modern insight into the full historicity of human existence, we now realize that to be human is to participate, however unequally, in the process by which women and men create themselves by creating their own societies and cultures. So far from being either divinely ordained or naturally given, even the most fundamental structures of social and cultural order are historically emergent, in that they are created, maintained, and/or transformed through human choice. This means that even these structures fall *within*, not outside, the sphere of human possibility and responsibility defined by God's universal saving grace. In other words, the good works necessary to our salvation include not only *works directed toward meeting needs arising within our established societies and cultures*, but also, and above all, *works directed toward changing these societies and cultures themselves*, so as to meet the still deeper human need for social and cultural orders that themselves are truly just, in that they permit all whose lives are determined by them a fair share in also determining them. To realize this, however, is to understand why the essential insight not only of the earlier "social gospel" but also of more recent "theologies of liberation" must necessarily find its place in any adequate doctrine of salvation. Even if one declines, as I do, to speak of "social salvation," because societies as such can neither sin nor be saved in the same sense in which only individual persons can, actually to live salvation includes and must include a life-praxis of liberation. By this I mean not only bearing explicit witness to all women and men of God's redemption of the world, and therefore of the real possibility of their own salvation from sin, but also bearing *implicit* witness to their salvation by, above all, actively working together with God and all other persons of good will for their emancipation, sharing fully in the conflict of human interests and taking sides in the struggle with the poor and the oppressed to build an ever freer and more equitable social and cultural order.

8

On the Last Things

8.1. THE "LAST THINGS" IN ORTHODOX THEOLOGY

THE TREATMENT OF ESCHATOLOGY in orthodox Protestant theologies commonly includes discussion of the following "last things" (*novissimis*; Greek: τὰ ἔσχατα):

1. the temporal death of the individual person (*mors*);

2. the resurrection of the dead (*mortuorum resurrectio*);

3. the last judgment (*extremum judicium*);

4. the end of the world (*consummatio sæculi*);

5. eternal life (*vita æterna*); and

6. eternal death (*mors æterna*).

These concepts-terms are typically interpreted in orthodox theologies as follows: After death the soul of the individual person, being immortal, lives on separated from the body. During the "intermediate state" (*status intermedius*) between its separation from the body and its reunification with the body at the time of the resurrection of the dead, the soul experiences a foretaste of either heaven or hell. The souls of the righteous during this interim are "in the hand of God" (*in manu Dei*) and await the fulfillment of eternal blessedness, while the souls of the godless find themselves "in the place of torment" (*in loco tormentorum*), where they await eternal damnation. Thereafter, at the appointed time, the bodies of all the dead are raised up, while those of all the living are transformed. The bodies of the righteous and of the godless alike are made "incorruptible" (*incorruptibilia*), and those of the righteous are, in addition, "transfigured," "empowered," and "spiritualized" (*clarificata, potentia, et spiritualia*). With the end of the world, wherewith all things other than human beings and angels are consumed by fire, Christ appears to hold the last judgment, assigning the righteous to eternal life, the godless to eternal death or damnation. Accordingly, of the five final "receptacles" (*receptacula*) traditionally distinguished by Roman Catholic theology—namely, "heaven" (*paradisus*), "hell" (*infernus*), "purgatory" (*purgatorium*), "limbo of infants" (*limbus infantium*), and "limbo of the fathers" (*limbus patrum*)—only the first two are validly distinguished. Also, eternal life, in which degrees or "grades" (*gradus*) are to be distinguished, consists, above all, in the "vision of God" (*visio Dei*). And in hell, which is eternal, there are likewise degrees or grades of torment (*gradus cruciatum*).

It will be understood, naturally, that in the case of this traditional doctrine of the last things, like all the other doctrines we have considered, there were nuances and variations in the ways in which individual thinkers developed it. But the main outlines, as I have briefly summarized them, have been followed again and again; and we may be assured that, if we orient ourselves to the scheme I have provided, we will not be seriously disadvantaged in approaching most of the treatments of the last things in orthodox Protestant—and, to a considerable extent, also Roman Catholic—theology.

But I do not propose to develop my own variation on this traditional pattern of themes—not, at any rate, in this discussion. My concern here, rather, is with the more fundamental question that I take to be necessarily presupposed by the traditional doctrine of last things as well as all other Christian doctrines—namely, what I have spoken of repeatedly as our existential question about the ultimate meaning of our existence as human beings. In my view, the deeper theme of eschatology, just as of the doctrines of God and of Jesus Christ and of every other doctrine, is the theme of our own human existence and all existence in its ultimate setting, which is to say, as grounded and ended in the pure, unbounded love of God and in God's gracious offer of salvation to all women and men. Because I am so confident about this, and because I am concerned that others, too, come to think about "the last things" in this light, I want to focus my argument on an exposition of the meaning of Christian hope—specifically, Christian hope in face of the "boundary situations" of transience and death, both as individuals and as a species. My conviction is that, if one can properly understand what Christians have been given the right and the power to hope for in the face of perishing and death—and what they are therefore called to attest as the hope in which every human being is given and called to share—then all of the details of a doctrine of "the last things"—of *all* the last things—either will pretty much take care of themselves or can be safely ignored. In their eschatology, above all, Christians have too often given their critics every reason to complain that they pretend to know more about the essential and irreducible mystery of human existence than anyone can rightly claim to know. In any case, I want to explicate in what follows how I understand the hope of which the writings of the New Testament and the church's tradition are the documentation, in the confidence that, by doing this, I can do as much as I am able to do to help focus our own eschatological reflection in the proper way.

8.2. THE MEANING OF CHRISTIAN HOPE

I begin by recalling briefly the characteristic features of Christian hope as it is classically attested by scripture and tradition. If we ask the writings of the New Testament what it is that Christians hope for, the answer at first glance seems clear enough. Christians hope for "the day of the Lord Jesus Christ," that is, for the "coming" or the "appearance" of Christ whereupon the final judgment and salvation of God will take place. Thus Paul writes to the Thessalonians, "the Lord himself will descend from heaven with a cry of command, with the archangel's call, and with the sound of the trumpet of God. And the dead in Christ will rise first; then we who are alive, who are left, shall be caught up together with them in the clouds to meet the Lord in the air; and so we shall always be with the Lord" (1 Thess 4:16–17). Implied by this hope is not only that, with the resurrection of the dead in Christ, the whole world will be judged and all human beings assigned to their final destination, but also that all this is going to happen soon—at any moment. But this is to say, in effect, that the hope attested by Paul, along with most of the other New Testament witnesses, is really only a christianization of the characteristic hope of late Jewish apocalyticism. The sole important difference is that, whereas Jewish hope looks forward to "the day of *God*" and to *God's* coming, Christian hope replaces this with the imminent coming of *the Lord Jesus* as God's Messiah.

In a few places in the New Testament, however, we encounter a very different way of formulating Christian hope. In part, certainly, because the original apocalyptic expectation of a near end of the world proved to be mistaken, but also because Christians more and more found themselves in a non-Jewish cultural and religious environment, the original apocalyptic hope tended to recede in favor of a more typically Hellenistic interpretation of human destiny. According to this interpretation, which seems to have been popularly represented by the important religious movement of Gnosticism, the decisive thing to come is not the end of the present age with the resurrection of the dead and the judgment of the entire world, but the death of each individual person, when, provided one is properly instructed and otherwise prepared, one ascends at once to the heavenly world of light whence one originally fell. In other words, whereas the apocalyptic hope is projected along the *horizontal* line of historical development and anticipates the resurrection of the body, the Gnostic hope is a *vertical* projection that envisages solely the immortality of the human soul. The chief witness to such a hope in the New Testament is the author of the Fourth Gospel, for whom the earlier apocalyptic hope expressed by Paul has completely lost its power. Although John, as we call him, fully retains the traditional Jewish belief in God's creation of the world, and thus rejects Gnostic dualism, including its doctrine of the self's pre-existence, the forms of his understanding of hope are taken straight out of Gnosticism. This is nowhere more evident than in the well-known words in the fourteenth chapter of his Gospel, which reflect the Gnostic picture of the soul's ascent upon death to reunite with its heavenly Redeemer: "In my Father's house are many dwelling places; if it were not so, would I have told you that I go to prepare a place for you? And when I go and prepare a place for you, I will come again and will take you to myself, that where I am you may be also" (John 14:2–3).

The striking thing, however, about the subsequent development of Christian witness and theology is that this Gnostic interpretation of hope did not generally displace the earlier Christian apocalypticism, as it clearly had in John's Gospel, but was simply superimposed upon apocalypticism to express the hope of Christian orthodoxy. As is indicated by the way it figures in the major Christian creeds, the apocalyptic hope for the resurrection of the dead more and more receded into the background of orthodox eschatology. Its foreground came to be held by something very like the Gnostic hope for immortality, which was believed to be fulfilled immediately upon the death of each individual person. Provided one had received the sacraments of the church and thus died in a state of grace, one could expect that one's soul would survive the death of one's body and be united at once with God in heaven. And yet, because the original apocalyptic picture of hope was never completely abandoned by the church, it continued to provide the larger setting, as it were, of traditional Christian doctrine. Even though the resurrection of the dead and the final judgment were now envisaged as events of the remote, rather than, as in most of the New Testament, of the immediate, future, the claim of the tradition was, and still is, that their occurrence alone will constitute the fulfillment of the whole of Christian hope.

Without supposing that this is more than the barest summary of the traditional hope of Christianity that orthodox theology, in its way, presupposes and develops, I would now make two observations about it.

First of all, given contemporary standards of meaning and truth, there can be no question that the concepts-terms in which Christian hope is classically attested are through and through mythological and must be interpreted accordingly. I do not mean by this that traditional Christian eschatology is simply false. The widespread popular assumption that what is mythological in its form of expression cannot be true evidences only the extent to which all of us today are, to some degree, under the spell of secularism. Underlying this assumption is the secularist denial that there is any truth other than the empirical truth most fully worked out in the sciences, from which it follows that, since mythology clearly cannot be taken as having a scientific kind of truth, one can only infer to its necessary falsity. Yet, even if one rejects this denial and the inference that follows from it, the fact remains that mythology cannot be construed as anything like science, even though it is the mark of mythological language to invite such misconstruction. Thus, in speaking as it does of the resurrection of the dead and of the last judgment, the myth of apocalypticism appears to refer to cosmic events of the near or distant future in something like the way in which the empirical language of science, also, might refer to "future events," such as those envisaged, say, by the second law of thermodynamics. On closer examination, however, it becomes evident that the use to which mythological language is actually put is quite different from the use of language—even the same language—in empirical science. The real intention of myth—and in this lies its distinctive kind of meaning and truth—is not to speak of any of the details of empirical reality in the manner of science, but rather to express our own most basic understanding of ourselves in relation to ultimate reality as a whole. Whereas, as R. G. Collingwood rightly argues, science by its very nature is concerned with the *parts* of reality, or with everything taken distributively, myth as the language of faith or religion is concerned with reality *as a whole*, and thus with everything taken collectively.[1] Because this is so, however, all mythology, and therefore the traditional language of Christian hope as well, has to be interpreted so that its real meaning and truth, so far as it has any, can be understood. In a word, the language of hope must be, as Rudolf Bultmann contends, *demythologized*. It must be interpreted in existentialist terms—in terms of its own real intention to disclose the meaning of our existence in relation to ultimate reality as a whole.[2]

And this leads to my second observation. The traditional mythology of Christian hope is, in fact, simply an amalgam of late Jewish apocalypticism and Gnosticism, and therefore as such nothing properly Christian, anyhow. Neither the collective hope for the final fulfillment of all creation nor the individual hope for the soul's ascent to heaven immediately after death is in the least original with Christianity, although both hopes, as we have seen, were adopted by Christians and eventually worked together into their traditional teaching about the last things. This is not to say, naturally, that there could not have been properly Christian reasons why Christians adopted these pictures of hope and retained them throughout the church's history. On the contrary, the Christian community almost certainly came to express its hope in these terms because, in addition to their being terms in which persons once naturally thought and spoke about themselves and the whole of reality of which they are a part, they were taken to be somehow appropriate to Christian hope itself. The point, however, is that *this hope is and must be the criterion for judging the mythology*—not the other way around. Even if the only way we today can expect to appropriate Christian hope is by interpreting its mythological forms of expression, it is nonetheless a *critical* appropriation that is called for if we are not simply to mistake Christian hope for something else. Recalling, then, my first observation that the language of hope, being mythological, has to be demythologized, or interpreted in terms of its understanding of human existence in relation to ultimate reality as a whole, we may now add that the criterion of our critical appropriation of it can only be the properly Christian understanding of our relation to God.

---

1. Collingwood, *Faith and Reason*, 122–47.
2. Bultmann, "Christian Hope and the Problem of Demythologizing."

If this is our theological task in the matter of eschatology, however, I hold that it cannot be all that difficult to accomplish. I do not mean, of course, that the essence of Christian hope is so obvious and simple that anything less than the most careful theological reflection could be sufficient to explicate it. My contention is simply that there can be no doubt as to the Christian understanding of our relation to God and therefore as to the criterion for interpreting Christian hope as well. So far as the Christian witness is concerned, the ultimate ground and object of our hope, even as of our faith and love, are precisely and only God Godself as decisively re-presented through Jesus Christ. This is to say that, for the Christian understanding of existence, the strictly ultimate reality to which we are all related is understood symbolically to be the pure, unbounded love whereby all fragmentary and transient lives are accepted and knit together into one integral and everlasting life. Even as this boundless love is at once the ultimate ground and object of our faith, of our obedient trust in reality and loyalty to it, so it is also the ultimate ground of our own capacity to love and the one inclusive object toward which all our love is to be directed. Being freed to love by God's prevenient love for us and for the whole creation, we are enabled to love both ourselves and all others in our returning love for God.

But, in the same way, the love of God is also the sole ultimate ground and object of Christian hope. Because what is ultimately real is not merely the world, but God's all-inclusive love of the world, there is a ground for hope beyond and in spite of the limits of the world itself with its transience and death. Although it is the destiny of the world and of everything in it that, having come to be, it should then perish and pass away, the world is nevertheless the good creation of God and the object of God's everlasting love. Thus whatever is created and emancipated is also redeemed and consummated, in the sense that it is fully embraced by God's love and there cherished forever for exactly what it is. But this means that God's love for us is itself the only ultimate *object* of Christian hope as well as its only ultimate *ground*. For while this hope is indeed the hope for a significance of ourselves and the world beyond and in spite of the limits of their own transience and death, *God's love alone* is sufficient to constitute their ultimate significance and therefore is itself not only *why* Christians hope but *what* they hope for as well.

In general, then, it is clear how a critical appropriation of traditional Christian mythology ought to proceed. Such mythology should be appropriated simply as the symbolic expression of Christian hope, of hope that is ultimately grounded in the love of God decisively re-presented through Jesus Christ and that is directed toward this selfsame love as its only ultimate object. Without going into all the details of such an appropriation, I would make two further points concerning it.

The first is that it would have no trouble at all agreeing that there are, in fact, properly Christian reasons for the church's traditional way of expressing its hope. Indeed, such an appropriation could readily explain why the pictures of hope of Jewish apocalypticism and Gnosticism could have both been adopted and retained by Christians in their witness and theology. The great virtue of apocalyticism, with its horizontal projection of hope and its central symbol of the resurrection of the body, is that it brings to expression the truly cosmic dimensions of Christian hope, which sees in the reality of God's love the promise of final fulfillment not only for each individual person and the whole of humankind, but also for literally every created thing. Even as the symbol of creation expresses that whatever is has its primal source solely in God's love, so the symbol of resurrection serves to affirm that it is in this same love of God that all things also have their only final end. Thus, even though the terms of apocalypticism are mythological, they may still be taken to affirm that the whole of history, including the larger history of nature, is everlastingly significant, and thus serve as fit symbols of Christianity's truly cosmic hope. What Christians ultimately hope for in hoping for God's endless love is nothing other or less than the new heaven and the new earth envisaged, in his way, by the author of the book of Revelation (21:1).

On the other hand, the merit of the Gnostic picture is to symbolize the meaning of Christian hope for each individual person. As surely as we human beings belong to nature and are continuous with it at every point, we are also distinguished within nature as the one place where, so far as we know, nature can become fully conscious of itself and of its primal source and final end. In fact, as we saw earlier in the discussion of human existence, it is this very capacity to be fully conscious of ourselves, and thus, in a way, of reality as a whole, that explains why we women and men are each said to be uniquely created in God's image, and therefore to be uniquely creatures of hope, even as we are also creatures who uniquely believe and love. Because of its projection of hope along the vertical and its central symbol of the immortality of the soul, Gnosticism, in its way, expresses this distinctiveness of human existence from the rest of nature.

Therefore, as mythological as it, too, certainly is, the Gnostic picture can still be taken as symbolizing the uniquely human relation to God, and thus of the meaning of Christian hope for human existence.

The second point I want to make, however, is that neither the apocalyptic hope for resurrection nor the Gnostic hope for immortality may be taken as anything other or more than a symbol of properly Christian hope—by which I mean, of course, hope in God's boundless love as itself the ultimate significance both of the world and of my own individual existence. Whether Christian hope is expressed in terms of the horizontal projection of apocalypticism, or expressed, rather, through the vertical projection of Gnosticism, it is in either case expressed in symbols that point beyond themselves. Since the reality of God's love, and hence the ultimate significance of our life, is neither simply one more event in the future out ahead of us nor real only in some heavenly realm up above us, both projections are inadequate to the real meaning of Christian hope. At best, they but provide pointers to its essential truth—that, in spite of the transience and death of all things, and even in spite of our own sinfulness as human beings, their and our final destiny is to be embraced everlastingly by God's love, and that we human beings, at least, can and should already share in this our eternal life in God through faith, hope, and love here and now in the present. In other words, the symbols of resurrection and immortality must be taken as pointing, not to some other life after this life but to *the everlasting significance of this life itself* in and through the boundless love of God. Which is to say that the only immortality or resurrection that is essential to Christian hope is not our own *subjective* survival of death, but our wholly *objective* immortality or resurrection in God, our being finally accepted and judged by God's love, and thus imperishably united with all creation into God's own unending life.

At this point, I cannot but think of two of my older contemporaries—one a philosopher, the other a theologian—whose thoughts closely converge with my own. The philosopher is Ludwig Wittgenstein, who, in a famous lecture on ethics, confesses to having sometimes had "the experience of feeling *absolutely* safe. I mean the state of mind," he explains, "in which one is inclined to say, 'I am safe, nothing can injure me, *whatever happens*.'"[3] Although Wittgenstein says little more about this feeling, or state of mind, it has always seemed very close to my own in hoping, as

---

3. "Wittgenstein's Lecture on Ethics," 8.

I do, for my objective immortality in God's love. The other thinker, who speaks in a remarkably similar way, is my friend, the New Testament scholar, Willi Marxsen. Toward the end of his book on the resurrection of Jesus, he recounts a story about his own theological teacher, Heinrich Rendtorff, who, when he was dying, asked his wife to listen quietly to what he had to say and then went on: "The last nights I have been thinking over and testing everything that we can know and everything that we have been told about what will happen to us when we die. And now I am certain of one thing: I will be safe." To which Marxsen adds: "Nobody could call Heinrich Rendtorff a representative of 'modern' theology. But he was a level-headed man who always tried to confine himself to statements which he could justify. The only thing he was sure of on his deathbed was: I shall be safe."[4]

To avoid any misunderstanding, I would add two further comments. Contrary to what some have seemed to think, I neither deny our subjective survival of death nor have the least interest in denying it, however problematic I continue to find all affirmations of it, especially affirmations of subjective immortality in the strict sense of the words, as distinct from merely subjective survival for a longer or shorter period after death. So far as my position involves any denial, it is the strictly *hermeneutical* denial that the expectation of such subjective survival or immortality is in any way essential to the hope that it is the business of a Christian doctrine of the last things to explicate and defend. Whether we do or do not subjectively survive death, what we hope for, insofar as our hope is *Christian* hope, is not our own subjective survival or immortality, but rather the utterly boundless and everlasting love of God for us and, because of it, our objective immortality or resurrection in and through God's love. In this, I cannot but think that I am applying yet again, in my own way, a favorite distinction of Luther's, who ever insists that the life we live, finally, is not "our own life" (*vita domestica*), but rather "another life" (*vita aliena*).

My second comment is this: I deeply believe that there is a strict *either/or* here that we must be ever careful not to ignore or obscure. Either our hope, finally, is in and for God, and in and for God *alone*, or else it is hope in and for something besides God, in which case it is an idolatrous hope that is unworthy of Christians. Unfortunately, the tradition of Christian witness and theology gives abundant evidence that the

4. Marxsen, *Resurrection of Jesus of Nazareth*, 188.

idolatry here can often be very subtle and refined. I always think, in this connection, of some of John Wesley's characteristic reflections on the end of human existence. On the one hand, he can speak eloquently of God as "the sole End, as well as the Source, of your being," and, on this basis, lay down the imperative, "Have no end, no ultimate end, but God." And yet, on the other hand, he can identify our only ultimate end, not as God Godself, but as our own "fruition" or "enjoyment" of God, or our own "happiness" in God.[5] But these, clearly, are two inconsistent answers to the question of the ultimate end of human life. If that end is our own enjoyment or happiness, even our enjoyment of, or our happiness in, God, then God Godself is not the sole end of our being but, at best, the means to its realization. Conversely, if the sole ultimate end of our life really is God Godself, then everything else, even our enjoyment of God or our happiness in God, is at best but a means to that one ultimate end. And so we are reminded yet again that it is, above all, in thinking and speaking about last things that Christians must never forget the watchword of all valid theology: *Soli Deo gloria!*

8.3. OVERCOMING SOME ANTITHESES IN TRADITIONAL ESCHATOLOGY

Continuing my argument that this is an appropriate as well as a credible interpretation of Christian hope, I now wish to point out how it also overcomes three familiar antitheses in traditional eschatological doctrine.

8.3.1. Present vs. Future

On the view I have just set forth, our redemption and consummation, and therefore our salvation, also, are evidently both present and future, things that are both already the case and yet still to be fully realized. Why? Well, because the redemption and consummation of all things are nothing other than their reception into the boundless love of God, which, in our human case, given the universal fact of sin, confronts us as also the promise and demand of salvation, as the unconditional acceptance of our lives into God's life, which gives and demands our acceptance of it through obedient faith. Although the always future event of God's love thus confronts us even now as gift and demand, it itself still remains always future as God's act of accepting our lives into God's own. There they have an

5. Wesley, *Standard Sermons*, vol. 1, 273–74.

abiding meaning or worth in spite of our own transience and death and in spite of the sin by which we again and again mistakenly and futilely try to overcome our own final insignificance in ourselves apart from God's all-accepting love for us. And this is the case quite aside from the question of our own subjective immortality or survival of death. For, however that question is resolved, whether we affirm our subjective immortality or, for good reasons, decline to do so, the final future for each of us is to be lovingly embraced into the everlasting life of God, thereby becoming objectively immortal in and through God's boundless love. And this future already confronts each of us here and now in the present as the gift and demand of saving grace—as the possibility and the responsibility of a new understanding of ourselves and the world in face of God's unconditional acceptance of all things. In other words, the continuity that the Christian witness undoubtedly affirms between the past and present, on the one hand, and the unending future, on the other, is the continuity established, not by *our* subjectivity but by *God's*—by God's redemption and consummation of the world, and, in our human case, by God's universal offer of salvation to all women and men, notwithstanding the fact of their sin.

8.3.2. *Individual vs. Cosmic Redemption-Consummation*

Every creature—not only every human being or understanding creature—is embraced by God's boundless love and thereby lives everlastingly in and through God's life as well as for it. The sole prerogative of the human creature, or of any other understanding creature there may be, is simply that she, he, or it can *understand* this, and thus understand her-, him- or itself and the world accordingly, as, presumably, none of the lower, nonunderstanding creatures is able to do. But because *each* creature individually is the object of God's love, *all* creatures collectively are nonetheless so—and vice versa. No individual is embraced by God's love except together with all the others, human and nonhuman, who are no less its beloved objects. And yet each individual is known, judged, and valued by that love for just the individual that she, he, or it uniquely is. Consequently, on the view I have set forth, neither the individual nor the cosmos can be played off against the other, and justice is done to the positive motives underlying both of the myths by which Christian hope has traditionally been expressed—the apocalyptic myth as well as the Gnostic myth.

I would draw particular attention, in this connection, to the fact that the doctrine of the last things that I have outlined more than meets the objection commonly made to Christianity by countless of its modern secular critics, that its hope for an ultimate future overcoming our transience and death as well as our sin diverts our proper concern and responsibility away from our present life here and now to some other life after it. On the view I have outlined, Christian hope in no way expresses hope for some other life after this life, but rather, as hope in God's all-embracing and everlasting love, expresses hope for *the abiding meaning of this life itself.* Therefore, so far from in any way compromising our proper concern for this world and our responsibility for working for its liberation from every form of bondage and oppression, for its emancipation no less than its redemption, Christian hope is disclosed to be the very best of reasons for having just such concern and responsibility. Just because it is hope for *God's* love, it is also hope for the *world's* ultimate significance in God, and this means that it is the kind of hope that issues in concerned and responsible action for the world's redemption and emancipation.

8.3.3. Double Destination vs. Universal Salvation

I already touched on this third antithesis briefly in my discussion of salvation. Here, too, there has traditionally been what I can only regard as a false choice. At issue in the assertion of double destination, of eternal life and eternal death, heaven and hell, are two important motives: (1) the unsurpassable righteousness of God, whose love is in no way oblivious to moral distinctions, but fully respects them; and (2) the freedom and responsibility of each woman or man to decide her or his own existence in face of the gift and demand of God's grace, and the everlasting meaning or significance of her or his decisions. On the other hand, the assertion of so-called universalism, or universal salvation, likewise expresses two important motives: (1) faith's unreserved confidence in God's unconditional love and grace, which are freely bestowed upon all, evil as well as good, sinners as well as righteous, and for the bestowal of which our moral goodness or righteousness is in no way a precondition; and (2) faith's no less unreserved confidence that, whatever the importance of a woman's or a man's decisions, *God's* decision is ultimately determinative, in that God is the final end as well as the primal source of all things and that our whole being, therefore, is in the nature of the case absolutely dependent and responsive, in no way independent and conclusive, any more than it is independent and originative. But on the view I have presented here, it is possible to do justice to all four of these legitimate motives, without ignoring or sacrificing any of them.

The reason for this is that the whole point of eschatology, as I have presented it, is to stress the all-encompassing love of God, which alone is the final end of all things—and, in a unique way, is the only final end of woman and man, since they each have the freedom and the responsibility to *understand* it as their final end and to exist accordingly already here and now in the present. But to recognize this basic point is to see the need for both readings of a single statement that together pick up the essential points of the two usual antithetical positions: (1) God loves *all things* exactly as they are, which is the essential point of universalism; and yet (2) God loves all things *exactly as they are*, which is the essential point of the counterposition of double destination. What we ourselves are and become, and so what we will be forever in God's all-loving judgment of us is, in part, what we ourselves decide to be in each present through our own responsible freedom. If we decide to open ourselves to God's grace in obedient faith, and thus in returning love for God and for all whom God loves, our neighbors as well as ourselves, then this is who we are and whom God judges and ever will judge us to be. If, on the other hand, we close ourselves against God and our fellow creatures, that, too, is who we are and whom God judges and ever will judge us to be to the farthest reaches of eternity. Nevertheless—and this is the countervailing truth in universalism—God's final judgment of us is nothing other than the judgment of God's pure, unbounded love, and so, whether or not we respond to God's grace in obedient faith working through love, we belong to God's love and to it alone as what finally determines the meaning and worth of our lives. In other words, although we may indeed live without authentic *faith* in God's love for us, we cannot live humanly at all without the *fact* of God's love for us—nor, as I feel bound to insist, without at least an *inauthentic* faith in it.

F. D. Maurice makes this point in what, for me, has proved an unforgettable way when he asks in a letter to his mother, "What, then, do I assert? Is there no difference between the believer and the unbeliever?" And then answers:

Yes, the greatest difference. But the difference is not about the *fact*, but precisely in the belief of the *fact*. God tells us, "In Him," that is in Christ, "I have created all things, whether they be in heaven or on earth. Christ is the Head of *every* [woman and] man." Some [women and] men believe this; some [women and] men disbelieve it. Those [women and] men who disbelieve it walk "after the flesh." They do not believe they are joined to an Almighty Lord of life,— One who is mightier than the world, the flesh, the devil,—One who is nearer to them than their own flesh. They do not believe this, and therefore they do not act upon this belief . . . But though tens of hundreds of thousands of [women and] men live after the flesh, yea, though every [woman and] man in the world were so living, we are forbidden by Christian truth and the Catholic Church to call this the real *state* of any [woman or] man . . . The truth is that every [woman and] man is in Christ; the condemnation of every [woman and] man is that [she or] he will not own the truth; [she or] he will not *act* as if this were *true*, [she or] he will not believe that which is the truth, that, except [she or] he were joined to Christ, [she or] he could not think, breathe, live a single hour.[6]

My conclusion, accordingly, is that any adequate Christian theology must affirm at least this much truth in universalism: in the spirit of Luther's insistence that the devil, after all, is God's devil, it must say that the hell of inauthentic existence is also God's hell. To say anything less than this would be to miss the whole point to which Paul bears witness in what must surely be the most powerful of all the statements about the last things ever made—his affirmation in Romans 8:38–39, that "neither death, nor life, nor angels, nor principalities, nor things present, nor things to come, nor powers, nor height, nor depth, nor anything else in all creation, will be able to separate us from the love of God in Christ Jesus our Lord."

6. Maurice, *Life of Frederick Denison Maurice*, vol. 1, 155.

9

Epilegomena: On Theology as a Christian Vocation

9.0. PRELIMINARY REMARKS

ESSENTIAL TO THIS BOOK from the argument of the first chapter on is the understanding that doing Christian theology is an integral part of the life-praxis of all Christians simply as such. To be called to be a Christian is to be called both to bear witness to Jesus Christ and, in order to bear it validly, to do Christian theology. Although, on the understanding of Christian faith for which I have argued, human beings are saved by grace alone through faith alone, I have underscored the point made by all Protestant theology that saving faith is never a "lonely faith," unaccompanied by good works, but is always rich in bearing fruit for the good of the creation and the glory of God. But if simply to be a Christian is, for this reason, also to do Christian theology, the converse statement is, on my understanding, false: simply to do Christian theology is *not*, necessarily, to be a Christian—any more than to do any other good work requires understanding oneself before God as we are given and called to do decisively through Jesus Christ.

In my view, then, doing Christian theology is one thing, doing Christian theology *as a Christian vocation*, something else—something more concrete and deserving of consideration in its own right, if only as the subject of "epilegomena," things said *in addition* to the things that have been said before. And I am all the clearer about this, considering that, in the future, even as in the past, the greater number of those who will actually do Christian theology—and for whom this book is especially intended—are sure to do it, in one sense or another, as a Christian vocation.

9.1. THE SENSES OF "VOCATION"

"Vocation" is simply the English word derived from the Latin word "*vocatio*" (from the infinitive, "*vocare*," to call), meaning the process of calling, or summoning. So I could just as well have entitled this chapter, "On Theology as a Christian Calling," and any reader preferring to do so may make the necessary substitutions.

As it happens, however, "vocation" is a systematically ambiguous term in the traditional vocabulary of Christian witness and theology because it acquires somewhat different senses in the different contexts in which it is used. There are, in fact, three distinct uses that need to be sorted out, beginning with what I take to be the first and, as it were, foundational, use.

As is clear simply from the word *ecclesia*, which we render in English with "church," Christians from the very beginning have understood themselves to be called out, just as they have understood Jesus Christ as the one through whom God has decisively called them out into the community of the church. But from a Christian standpoint, Christians as those whom God has decisively called are by no means alone in having been called by God. On the contrary, the decisively called are understood to belong to an indefinitely larger and more inclusive community of the called, comprising the implicitly called as well as those who have been called explicitly.

Any being who is human is one of the *implicitly* called as soon and as long as she or he is human at all—being human and being at least implicitly called being simply two ways of saying the same thing. But, then, any human being who is in any way religious or for whom the claim of some religion to be true is a genuine option is one of the *explicitly* called as soon and as long as she or he is religious in any way at all or has a genuine option of becoming such—being religious in some way or having a genuine option of becoming such and being explicitly called by God being simply two ways of saying the same thing.

In an analogous way, any human being who is somehow Christian or for whom the claim of the Christian religion to be true is a genuine option is one of the *decisively* called as soon and as long as she or he is a Christian or has a genuine option of becoming such, being in some way a Christian or having the option of becoming a Christian and being decisively called by God being—on the Christian understanding—simply two ways of saying the same thing.

But wherein, exactly, does one's being one of the decisively called of God consist? It does not consist merely in one's being called to authentic existence in relation to God as well as oneself and the world, since both the implicitly called and the explicitly called are, in their respectively different ways, also called to that. Being decisively called consists, rather, in one's being called to exist authentically *in a very specific way*—namely, through both the effective use and the valid administration of the specifically Christian means of salvation, which is to say, not only such secondary means as word, sacrament, and ministry, or even the primary means that is the visible church as such, but also the primal means that is Jesus Christ himself. To be decisively called is to be called to exist authentically through effectively using Jesus Christ and the visible church as well as all that represents them in the way in which God intends that they be used—namely, through *faith*, and then to join in the general ministry of validly administering these same means of salvation to others, so that they, too, may effectively use them—namely, through *good works*, or, as I usually say, through bearing witness, implicit as well as explicit.

So much for the first or foundational sense of "vocation" in which it means the calling to authentic existence through being a Christian that is issued through Jesus Christ and the witness of the visible church through its means of salvation. A second sense of the term has to do, not with this call to be a Christian, and thus to the *general* ministry to which each and every Christian is ordained by her or his baptism, but with a call to the *special* ministry, i.e., the representative ministry, of the visible church.

Such a call to the special ministry has been helpfully analyzed as involving three main elements in addition to the call to the general ministry issued to all Christians, which the special call presupposes: (1) the *secret* call to the individual person; (2) the *providential* call confirming that she or he has the requisite gifts and graces, knowledge and skills; and (3) the *ecclesial* call whereby the visible church, recognizing the validity of the person's general, secret, and providential calls, explicitly and publicly ordains her or him to its representative ministry.[1] Although the paradigm case here, obviously, is the ordained ministry, the essential point can be generalized to cover any and all special ministries in the church, ordained or not, provided they involve an official ecclesial call. In any event, the essential difference between vocation in the first or foundational sense

---

1. Niebuhr, *Purpose of the Church and Its Ministry*, 64.

of the call to Christian existence and vocation in the second sense of the call to the special ministry of the visible church is that the first comes to each and every Christian simply as such, whereas the second comes to only some Christians, depending on their individual differences from other members of the community, including, especially, their aptitude for leadership of the church.

This leads naturally to the third sense of "vocation," which has been especially important in the tradition of the churches of the Protestant Reformation. In this sense, "vocation" has to do neither with the calling to Christian existence and the general ministry of bearing witness nor with the calling to the special ministry of leading the visible church. It has to do, instead, with the calling to do whatever one does in the world in the way of one's lifework as likewise a special ministry, in the sense of a special service to God in and through one's service to those of whom God is preeminently the servant. Provided that the work one does in the world serves in one way or another to enable the world's fulfillment to the glory of God, it, too, is a special ministry just as much as, and in no way essentially different from, the representative ministry of the church. On a Reformation understanding, the fundamental decisions that all human beings have to make with respect to marital status and type of lifework are exactly analogous to the decisions faced by anyone called to the representative ministry of the visible church; and they, too, need to listen for God's call to *their* work, not only on the basis of their general call as Christians and in their secret call as individual persons, but, above all, in their providential call and in some kind of an official call, even though it is not an ecclesial call issued by the visible church.

But if on the understanding of Reformation Christianity, all types of lifework that genuinely serve God's cause in the world, even the so-called secular ones, are, in their ways, sacred callings from God Godself, it is equally true that all callings, even so-called sacred ones, are in themselves thoroughly secular—in that they are one and all ways of working in this world, or in this age (*sæculum*), that perforce rely upon the same worldly means to accomplish their ends.

9.2. DOING THEOLOGY AS A CHRISTIAN VOCATION

Now when I speak of doing theology as a Christian vocation, it is not the first or foundational sense of "vocation" that I mainly have in mind, but rather its second and third senses. To be sure, we saw already in chapter 1 that there is a profound and very important sense in which each and every Christian believer is called to be a lay theologian. If, as we have also seen, to be decisively called, on a Christian understanding, is to be called both to use effectively and to administer validly the specifically Christian means of salvation, one can carry out one's primary obligation to bear a valid Christian witness only insofar as one critically reflects on the meaning and validity of what one thinks, says, and does as a Christian, together with everything else that is thought, said, and done by one's sisters and brothers in the church. Thus to reflect, however, on the meaning and validity of bearing Christian witness is exactly what it means to do Christian theology, whether one concerns oneself, as the systematic theologian does, especially with the claim of bearing witness to be adequate to its content, and thus to be both appropriate to Jesus Christ and credible to human existence, or whether one's special concern is the practical theologian's with the other claim of bearing witness to be fitting to its situation. But if being called to be a theologian in this general sense is already necessarily implied simply in being called to be a Christian, and thus to the general ministry of the visible church, this is not the sense in which doing theology is *a* Christian vocation. This it is only in the sense that, among the special callings to which individual Christians may be called as their type of lifework, there is the special calling of leading in the church's necessary task of self-criticism, by critically reflecting on the meaning and validity of bearing Christian witness. Indeed, the special calling to lead in such critical reflection is already necessarily implied by any special calling to the representative ministry. As a leader in the church's task of bearing witness to the world, the representative minister must also be a leader in the church's theological task of critically reflecting on the meaning and validity of its witness, but for which its validity cannot possibly be secured.

But if a vocation to do theology is thus necessarily implied by any vocation to representative ministry, one need not be specially called to the ministry in order to have a special calling to be a Christian theologian. One may be called to be a theologian by a secret call to devote one's lifework to reflecting critically on the meaning and validity of bearing Christian witness and by then having this call validated both providentially, by possessing the gifts and graces necessary for acquiring the requisite knowledge and skills, and officially, by being called to exercise one's ability by some appropriate institution, whether a college, a university, or a school of theology.

As I see them, then, practicing ministry and doing theology are each to be analyzed in much the same way in terms of two levels and two forms. There are two levels of practicing ministry: *general* and *special*; and there are two forms of practicing special ministry: *generalized* and *specialized*. Similarly, there are two levels of doing theology: *lay* and *professional*; and there are two forms of doing professional theology: *ecclesial* and *academic*.

By doing theology as a Christian vocation, then, I mean doing theology at the professional, as distinct from the lay, level, in either the ecclesial or the academic form. In its ecclesial form, the immediate context of doing professional theology is the church and the ongoing process of bearing Christian witness, which can continue to go on validly only by means of critical reflection on its meaning and validity. In its academic form, by contrast, the immediate context of doing theology professionally is the academy and the ongoing process of theological reflection itself, which can continue to go on only by means of theological research, scholarship, and teaching. Thus the ecclesial theologian typically pursues her or his theological questions more for the sake of the answers, for which, as a representative minister, she or he always has more or less urgent practical need. The academic theologian, on the other hand, typically pursues her or his theological questions more for the sake of the questions themselves, in the sense of learning how to refine them and the methods for answering them, so that the process of theological inquiry can become ever more adequate and fruitful in its results. I put this difference as a matter of more or less, however, because it is a relative, not an absolute, difference. Just as the academic theologian ought never to forget that the only justification, finally, for her or his critical reflection is the process of bearing valid Christian witness of which it is but the servant, so the ecclesial theologian ought always to remember that her or his reflection can perform its distinctive service only if it remains sufficiently independent of the church's witness to be critical reflection on it and therefore of only indirect service to it.

In either form, however, professional theology ought to be precisely that, and nothing less. Thus, whenever I hear one of my former students introduce a statement by some such disclaimer as, "Of course, I'm not a professional theologian, but . . . ," I always feel obliged to remind her or him of the responsibility that she or he has disavowed. "You may not be an *academic* theologian, all right. But unless and until you return your MDiv diploma, I, for one, intend to hold you accountable for being the *ecclesial* and, therefore, *professional* theologian you affected to be in accepting it."

But now the fact that the ecclesial theologian and the academic theologian are alike professionals means that they are both engaged on the same level, even if in their respectively different forms, in the same process of reflecting critically on the meaning of bearing Christian witness and on the validity of the claims that it makes or implies. Whatever else this means, it certainly means that both pursue their questions in a deliberate, methodical, and reasoned way, and thus as participants in an established field of critical reflection having its own aims and explanatory ideals, its own "genealogy of problems," and its own ever-changing population of concepts and terms wherewith to formulate its problems and its proposals for solving them, not to mention its own professional associations and organs of peer review, including journals and other publications. In other words, critical reflection is one thing, the kind of deliberate, methodical, and reasoned critical reflection constitutive of the professional level of rational inquiry, something else. And this explains why both forms of professional theology naturally presuppose theological education, in the sense of a more or less formal process of teaching and learning, instruction and training, without which no one could become a professional theologian in either of the two forms.

Of course, by "*theological* education" here, I mean something other than "*religious* education," or, more exactly, "*Christian* education." If Christian education properly consists in such instruction and training as may be necessary in order for one to exist and act as a Christian by both effectively using the Christian witness and validly bearing it, the objective of theological education is distinctively different. It is, quite simply, to develop an operational competence in critically reflecting on Christian witness so as to interpret its meaning and to validate its claims to validity. So, although theological instruction and training may very well serve indirectly to develop a Christian self-understanding and life-praxis, their direct object is to impart the knowledge and skills that are necessary to critically reflecting, at a professional level, on the meaning of Christian witness and on the claims to validity that bearing it either makes or implies.

9.3. OTHER FEATURES OF CHRISTIAN VOCATIONS

But if both forms of doing Christian theology professionally necessarily presuppose the same kind of advanced, as distinct from basic, theological education; and if it, in turn, depends on the same underlying process of theological research, scholarship, and teaching, this is not all they have in common insofar as they are pursued as specifically Christian vocations. In fact, they share in all the other features that characterize any Christian vocation simply as such. Thus, whether one is an ecclesial theologian, as most theological students are preparing to be, or whether one is an academic theologian, as some of them go on to become, one's vocation is, in several important features, exactly the same as any other Christian vocation in the second and third senses of the term.

This is true, first of all, in that one's lifework as a theologian, whether ecclesial or academic, is supposed to serve the same ulterior end served somehow by all other Christian vocations. Simply put, this end is the fullest possible realization of the potentialities of the creation as the indispensable means to the glory of God. God is decisively re-presented to us through Jesus Christ as the pure, unbounded love whose own good is inclusive of the good of all the many creatures of this love—both individually and collectively. This is why, as we have seen, we can be commanded to love the Lord our God with all our heart, mind, soul, and strength and yet be commanded to love our neighbors as ourselves. Because God has always already identified Godself with ourselves and our neighbors, our love for our neighbors as ourselves is nothing alongside of, or merely additional to, our love for God, but is included in this very love. In fact, far from being a diversion of at least part of our love away from God to something else, loving our neighbors as ourselves is the only way in which we can love God Godself. But to love another is always to seek the good of the other, and this always means to do justice, to see to it that what properly belongs to the other actually goes to her or him and not to someone else. By our time in human history, this root meaning of justice has been clearly disclosed to have a specifically political aspect in that we now realize that not only our individual acts but also the basic structures of society and culture themselves all fall within the scope of human freedom and responsibility. Thus one of the things that belongs most fundamentally to the good of any creature—that it be able to live in a world sufficiently ordered to allow it to be and to become itself in solidarity with others—

is now seen to be something for which we ourselves are responsible, insofar, at least, as the structures of society and culture are essential parts of such an ordered world. Thus not only are all acts of Christians supposed to be directed toward the end of love and, therefore, to the doing of justice, but they must also be directed toward the achievement of social and cultural justice, in the sense of achieving, so far as possible, just structures of society and culture.

This, of course, is the insight first worked out by the witness and theology of the social gospel, only then to be self-critically revised and developed by so-called neo-orthodox theologians such as Reinhold Niebuhr into some form or other of "Christian realism," and finally to emerge more recently in generally more idealistic, even utopian, forms in certain political theologies and theologies of liberation. According to the typical expressions of this insight in contemporary theology, the work of the theologian as the "second act" of more or less critical reflection on the "first act" of liberating praxis is by its very nature directed to the end of achieving social and cultural justice, and thus to liberating all who are now oppressed by the unjust structures of existing society and culture. My only quarrel with this claim is that it is made about doing theology itself and as such, instead of about doing theology *as a Christian vocation*—in essentially the same way in which it was claimed by certain Americans during the Cold War that basic research in nuclear physics was to be directed toward constantly improving the United States' arsenal of weapons vis-à-vis the Soviet Union. No doubt, doing nuclear physics *as a committed anti-Communist* would have entailed doing it with just such an end in view. But it was this kind of existential commitment that would have given research in nuclear physics such an ulterior end, not such research in and of itself. In somewhat the same way, it is the Christian commitment of the theologian, insofar as there is, in fact, such a commitment, that accounts for the theologian's serving the ulterior end of love and justice, including justice in its political aspect. My first point, however, is that this is exactly how it should be. Doing theology quite properly serves the same ulterior end that any other Christian vocation is supposed to serve insofar as it is done on the basis of one's calling to be a Christian.

But one's lifework as a theologian—and this is a second feature it shares with any other Christian vocation—can serve this ulterior end only insofar as it is devoted, utterly and completely, to doing what Christian theology is supposed to do. On the understanding of theology for which I have argued, and have tried to practice throughout the book, what Christian theology is supposed to do, and the *only* thing it is supposed to do, is so to reflect critically on the meaning of bearing Christian witness and its two claims to be adequate to its content and fitting to its situation as to be able to validate these claims critically. Accordingly, as I understand the proper work of the Christian theologian, the only way in which she or he as such, as a theologian, can serve the ulterior end of love seeking justice is by engaging in just this kind of critical reflection in the deliberate, methodical, and reasoned way that the professional theologian, ecclesial or academic, is committed to do. I stress the theologian *as a theologian* because the word "theologian" properly refers to an *office*, not to a *person*. Of course, only a person can fill the office, even as persons alone are able to fill any of the other offices that God calls human beings to fill. But just as it would be wrong simply to identify a woman with her office as wife or mother, or a man with his office as husband or father, so it would be equally wrong simply to identify any person with her or his office as a theologian. Any such person, being involved in the complex sets of relationships distinctive of human life as we know it, will be not only a theologian but many other things besides, in the sense that she or he will have any number of offices to fill, the respective demands of which not only can be, but often are, more or less seriously conflicting. But insofar as one's vocation as a Christian is to do the critical reflection that is Christian theology, the only way in which one can serve the ulterior end of loving one's neighbor as oneself in one's love of God is by doing the best job one can do at just such critical reflection—in much the same way that a Christian whose vocation is to practice medicine can serve the same ulterior end of love seeking justice only by being the most knowledgeable and skilled medical practitioner that she or he is capable of being.

To be sure, we saw in Chapter 1 that one of the interesting things about being a theologian is that what it properly means to be one is itself a theological question that a theologian as such is responsible for asking and answering. The medical professional no doubt has to ask an analogous question about what it properly means to practice medicine if she or he is really to perform at a professional level. But the question about what it properly means to be a medical practitioner or theoretician is not a question of medicine, but a question, rather, of the *philosophy* of medicine; and it is only in another capacity, as a philosopher of medicine, that the medical professional or anyone else can answer it. It is otherwise, however, with the professional theologian, who, like the philosopher, has no one to turn to but her- or himself, or to her or his fellow theologians, in order to answer the question about the nature and task of theology, and hence about what she or he is supposed to be doing. The difficulty, of course, is that this theological question, exactly like any other, always arises in some particular historical situation and therefore can be neither formulated nor answered except in the terms, and so within the limits, of this situation and such opportunities as it may offer. So just what the theologian is supposed to be doing can never be determined once-for-all, but must be continually determined anew by critical theological reflection. Moreover, the field of Christian theology, as it is established at any given time, is like any other social or cultural structure, in that it reflects the same biases and injustices that are otherwise evident in society and culture generally—witness the fact that, until very recently, indeed, Christian theology has been so established that doing it has been a serious vocational choice exclusively for white, middle-class males. My point, then, in saying that the only way the theologian as such can serve the ulterior end of all Christian vocations, of love seeking justice, is by doing theology is not at all to say that she or he can only do what the theologian is conventionally supposed to do, given the social and cultural, including the ecclesial and theological, *status quo.* On the contrary, in my view, the theologian is accountable *precisely as a theologian* for a thoroughly critical understanding of doing theology as well as for a praxis of theology that is informed by such an understanding. Even so, the point stands, I think, that, if the theologian *as theologian* is to serve the end that all Christian vocations are supposed to serve, she or he can do nothing other than the best job possible at the kind of critical reflection on the meaning and validity of bearing Christian witness that Christian theology exists to do.

This leads naturally to yet a third feature that doing theology as a Christian vocation fully shares with any other Christian calling—namely, that doing theology professionally, whether as an ecclesial or as an academic theologian, involves one in the same paradox of sacred and secular that characterizes all Christian vocations. If one can serve love and justice as a theologian only by doing what theology exists to do, what theology exists to do is the work of critical reflection that is just as sacred and just as secular as any other human work—no more and no less. I recall what I said earlier about the important changes made in the understanding of Christian vocations by the Protestant Reformers. Whereas, for medieval

Catholicism, the concept "vocation" was restricted to cases where persons were called to the special, representative ministry or to the "religious," which is to say, the monastic, life of monk or nun, for the Reformers, it was understood to apply to any and all forms of human lifework in the world, provided only that they served the end of preserving and fulfilling creation to the greater glory of God. Thus, whatever the nature of one's work, it is thoroughly sacred only in the final end it serves, even while being thoroughly secular in the means it employs in the service of this end.

Luther typically made this point by insisting that there are no holy places in the world, the whole of which is profane, notwithstanding that "the earth everywhere is the Lord's." In other words, the holiness of the world, as he liked to say, is not "domestic," something belonging to it as its own, but rather "alien," something belonging to it thanks solely to the grace of another, the God whose love alone is holy in itself and alone makes anything else holy that can be validly said to be so. Thus, as Bultmann rightly argues, it is not the ordination of the priest that makes the church holy, but solely the word of God's love insofar as it is rightly proclaimed through the church's preaching and sacraments.[2]

This same paradox of holy and profane, sacred and secular, characterizes doing theology as a Christian vocation. As sacred as it is when judged by the end it exists to serve, it itself is as utterly secular as anything else a human being could possibly do as a calling from God. This means, for one thing, that theological thinking is not some peculiar kind of thinking requiring special qualifications of theologians or special criteria for theological claims. Rather, theological thinking is nothing other than the same critical reflection that is involved in any other process of interpreting the meaning of what we ordinarily think, say, and do in our life-praxis as human beings and then validating the claims to validity that we thereby make or imply. Just as validity is one, so the critical reflection necessary to determine validity is also one; and this is so even though the domains of validity, and their respective criteria, are indeed many, corresponding to the many different ways in which we human beings can lay claim to validity with or without good reasons to do so. This means, among other things, that the nonmoral excellences, the knowledge and skills, that are required in order to be a theologian can and must be learned in exactly

---

2. Bultmann, *New Testament and Mythology and Other Basic Writings*, 122–23.

the same secular way in which any other human knowledge and skills can and must be learned.

But it also means that, if there are indeed reasons for a Christian to think and say, "Theology is prayer," there is neither more nor less reason to do so than to make an equivalent statement about any other form of useful human work—such as, e.g., "Homemaking is prayer," or "Garbage collecting is prayer." All Christians are familiar with the New Testament admonitions that they are to pray without ceasing; and they know that some among them, and certainly some of their forebears, have understood these admonitions to mean that they were to be continually engaged around the clock in some form or other of religious exercise, public or private. But if we consider these admonitions as we should, in their actual context, it seems clear that we understand them correctly only if we look upon all that Christians are to think, say, or do, whether religious or secular, as service of God through service of those whom God loves, and, in this sense, as prayer, or as what Paul calls in Romans 12 our "rational worship." Thus, as true as it may be that theology is indeed prayer, this is in no way peculiarly true of theology but can be said just as truly of any other form of lifework that is also service of God because, or insofar as, it is service of the creatures who are all embraced by God's boundless love. I feel bound to add that the dangers of saying, "Theology is prayer" seem to me to be sufficiently great that one perhaps ought not to say it at all without making clear in doing so that, in respect of this, as well as all the other features I have mentioned, doing theology is in no way different from any other Christian vocation.

9.4. CONCLUSION

In any event, the last thought I want to leave with the reader, somewhat in the way in which others have thought to say summarily "Theology is prayer," is that *theology is critical reflection.* I trust I have said enough to make clear that I do not understand my statement to be in any way contrary to theirs, provided only that "prayer" is taken in the broad sense of service of God and therefore can be equally well applied to any form of such service, whether secular or religious. But if the two statements need not be inconsistent, they certainly express different emphases.

On my understanding, such dangers as there may be in insisting that theology is critical reflection—especially to students of theology—pale in comparison with the dangers of making the other statement. For a whole variety of reasons, at least some of which I should myself regard as good ones, the greatest temptation to which most of us continue to be exposed in thinking of theology is not too sharply differentiating it from prayer, or from faith and bearing witness in general, but too simply identifying it with them. Thus the proper dialectic between actually existing as a Christian and bearing witness, on the one hand, and critically reflecting on the meaning and validity of doing so, on the other—this dialectic most commonly breaks down because the difference between its two poles is collapsed.

Of course, the history of theology exhibits at least some instances of the dialectic breaking down in the other direction, insofar as doing theology has sometimes become so estranged from the witness on which it is supposed to reflect that it has effectively ceased to be of even indirect service to validly bearing the witness. But, as I read this long history, this way of theology's going wrong has never been anything like as common as the opposite way, the way of so assimilating doing theology to the bearing witness on which it has the task of reflecting that the only service it is in a position to provide is anything but *critical* reflection. The conclusive evidence for this, I believe, is the long struggle in the church that continues right up to our own time for theological freedom, for the freedom to reflect theologically in a thoroughly critical way. This struggle goes on not only in the Roman Catholic Church, but also in the Protestant churches, where the faculty and students of their theological schools are again and again so intimidated by the outside pressures of groups and individuals that they cannot think theologically at all, except with the kind of siege mentality that those familiar with the recent situation in many Protestant seminaries will have had ample opportunity to experience. In short, the greatest danger to doing theology, as I understand it, is that it will not be sufficiently established in its difference from the faith and bearing witness on which it reflects that it can perform the service that critical reflection alone is in a position to perform. But if I am right about this, nothing can be more important for me to say at the conclusion of our reflections together than that theology is critical reflection, and that any reflection that is not thoroughly critical neither is nor can be theology in the sense in which I have explained and tried to practice it throughout this book.

I deliberately qualify my point in this way because I readily grant that this is not the only sense in which "theology" has been, and can be, properly used. In the literal, etymological meaning of the word, according to which, as *logos* about *theos*, it means simply thought and/or speech about God, "theology" can be used in much the same sense in which I have used the term "witness," or, at any rate, "explicit witness." Nor do I have any objection to its being used in this very broad sense, provided this is not assumed to be either its only or its most distinctive meaning. Still, whatever terms we use to describe them, there remains the rock-bottom, fundamental difference between *making or implying claims to validity*, as one cannot fail to do in what I mean by bearing Christian witness, and *critically reflecting* on the meaning of such witness and the validity of its claims, as one is called to do in what I mean by doing Christian theology.

Furthermore, it belongs to the very nature of the church's mission to bear valid witness to Jesus Christ that it is always involved, and should be involved, in doing both of these things—both making or implying the claim to bear a valid Christian witness and, in order to make good on this claim, also critically reflecting on its witness so as to determine what it really means and whether or not it is really valid. What is at stake for me in insisting that theology is critical reflection is simply that the church's primary obligation to bear witness cannot possibly be carried out, except by sheer accident, unless it meets its secondary obligation so to reflect critically on its witness as to do all that human effort is able to do to make sure that its witness is, in fact, as valid as it claims to be.

"There are varieties of gifts," Paul says, "but the same Spirit; and there are varieties of service, but the same Lord; and there are varieties of working, but it is the same God who inspires them all in every one" (1 Cor 12:1–11). If what I have said in this chapter is correct, the critical reflection that is theology represents the cultivation of one of the Spirit's gifts, even as it performs one form of the Lord's service, and is one of the ways of working of which God is the inspiration. Consequently, I have no hesitation in speaking of the theologian who fills her or his office as a Christian vocation as "servant of the servants of God." From at least the time of Gregory the Great, this title has been applied to the office of Pope as primate of the universal church; and an appropriate title it is, considering the saying of Jesus in the gospels that, "If any one would be first, [she or] he must be last of all and servant of all" (Mark 9:35). The title is applied just as properly, however, to any other office of special ministry, high or low, if one holds, as I do, that the whole point of any such office is in one way or another to be of service to the servants of God who constitute the general ministry of the visible church. But if this concluding part of my argument is sound, the title is just as appropriate for the office of the professional theologian, whether ecclesial or academic. Although in this case the service of God's servants can never be more than the indirect service of critical reflection, it alone can make good their claim to fulfill their servant task by bearing a valid witness to Jesus Christ.

Bibliography

Atkinson, James, editor. *Luther's Works*. Vol. 44: *The Christian in Society I*. Philadelphia: Fortress, 1966.

Bonhoeffer, Dietrich. *Ethics*. Translated by N. H. Smith. London: SCM, 1965.

Brooke, Stopford A., editor. *Life and Letters of Frederick W. Robertson, M.A.* Vol. 2. New ed. London: Smith, Elender, 1868.

Bultmann, Rudolf. "The Christian Hope and the Problem of Demythologizing." *Expository Times* 65 (1954) 228–30; 276–78.

———. *New Testament and Mythology and Other Basic Writings*. Edited and translated by Schubert M. Ogden. Philadelphia: Fortress, 1984.

Collingwood, R. G. *Faith and Reason: Essays in the Philosophy of Religion*. Edited by Lionel Rubinoff. Chicago: Quadrangle, 1968.

Dolan, John Patrick, editor. *Unity and Reform: Selected Writings of Nicholas de Cusa*. Notre Dame, IN: University of Notre Dame Press, 1962.

Elliott, T. S. *Murder in the Cathedral*. New York: Harcourt Brace, 1935.

Hartshorne, Charles. "Two Forms of Idolatry." *International Journal for Philosophy of Religion* 1.1 (1970) 3–15.

Heppe, Heinrich. *Reformed Dogmatics: Set Out and Illustrated from the Sources*. Foreword by Karl Barth. Revised and edited by Ernst Bizer. Translated by G. T. Thomson. London: Allen & Unwin, 1950.

Inge, W. R. *Things New and Old: Sermons and Addresses in Great St. Mary's Cambridge, January 28th to February 5th, 1933*. London: Longmans, Green, 1933.

James, William. *Some Problems of Philosophy: A Beginning of an Introduction to Philosophy*. New York: Longmans, Green, 1911.

Knox, John. *The Early Church and the Coming Great Church*. Nashville: Abingdon, 1955.

Macquarrie, John. *Principles of Christian Theology*. 2nd ed. New York: Scribner, 1977.

Marxsen, Willi. *Jesus and Easter: Did God Raise the Historical Jesus from the Dead?* Translated by Victor Paul Furnish. Nashville: Abingdon, 1990.

———. *The Resurrection of Jesus of Nazareth*. Translated by Margaret Kohl. Philadelphia: Fortress, 1970.

Maurice, Frederick, editor. *The Life of Frederick Denison Maurice: Chiefly Told in His Own Letters*. Vol. 1. New York: Scribner, 1884.

Maurice, Frederick Denison. *Theological Essays*. New York: Harper & Brothers, 1957.

Bibliography

Niebuhr, H. Richard. *The Meaning of Revelation*. New York: Macmillan, 1941.

———. *The Purpose of the Church and Its Ministry: Reflections on the Aim of Theological Education*. New York: Harper & Brothers, 1956.

Ogden, Schubert M. *Faith and Freedom: Toward a Theology of Liberation*. 2nd rev. and enlarged ed. 1989. Reprinted, Eugene, OR: Wipf & Stock, 2005.

———. *Is There Only One True Religion or Are There Many?* Dallas: Southern Methodist University Press, 1992.

———. *On Theology*. 1986. Reprinted, Dallas: Southern Methodist University Press, 1992.

———. *The Point of Christology*. 1982. Reprinted, Dallas: Southern Methodist University Press, 1992.

———. *The Reality of God and Other Essays*. 1966. Paperback edition with new Preface, 1977. Reprinted, Dallas: Southern Methodist University Press, 1992.

Oman, John. *Vision and Authority: Or the Throne of St. Peter*. London: Hodder & Stoughton, 1902.

Outler, Albert C., editor. *The Works of John Wesley*. Vol. 2: *Sermons II*. Nashville: Abingdon, 1985.

Rahner, Karl. *The Christian of the Future*. Translated by W. J. O'Hara. Quaestiones disputatae 18. New York: Herder & Herder, 1967.

Schmid, Heinrich. *The Doctrinal Theology of the Evangelical Lutheran Church*. 3rd ed. Translated by Charles A. Hay and Henry E. Jacobs. Minneapolis: Augsburg, 1961.

Segundo, Juan Luis. *The Community Called Church*. Translated by John Drury. Maryknoll, NY: Orbis, 1973.

Tillich, Paul. *The Shaking of the Foundations*. New York: Scribner, 1948.

———. *Systematic Theology*. Vol. 2: *Existence and the Christ*. Chicago: University of Chicago Press, 1957.

Vidler, Alec R. *The Theology of F. D. Maurice*. London: SCM, 1948.

Wesley, John. *Standard Sermons*. Vol 1. Edited by Edward H. Sugden. 3rd ed. London: Epworth, 1951.

Wiles, Maurice. *Working Papers in Doctrine*. London: SCM, 1976.

Wittgenstein, Ludwig. "Wittgenstein's Lecture on Ethics." *Philosophical Review* 74.1 (1965) 3–12.

Scripture Index

Scripture Index

Subject and Name Index